Dare to be Different

(A Handbook on Practical Management Insights)

Narendar V. Rao
and
D. Vasudeva Rao

Library of Congress Control Number:		2023917454
ISBN:	Hardcover	979-8-3694-0739-4
	Softcover	979-8-3694-0738-7
	eBook	979-8-3694-0737-0

Print information available on the last page.

Rev. date: 09/22/2023

To order additional copies of this book, contact:
Xlibris
844-714-8691
www.Xlibris.com
Orders@Xlibris.com
850605

Contents

Dedication

This book is dedicated to the memory of my father, Mr. D. Vasudeva Rao. He was a soft-spoken, unassuming gentleman with a passion for excellence. He rose from humble beginnings to become the managing director of India's preeminent automobile jobbing foundry at that time—Ennore Foundries Ltd. (EFL). He had a very humanistic approach to management. He believed that the most critical part of the organization are the employees. Hence, he created unique welfare schemes for their benefit and designed innovative training programs to equip them with the technical and soft skills necessary to succeed in an increasingly competitive global business environment. He was indeed an exceedingly rare human being who inspired me to excel in everything that I do.

Acknowledgments

The authors wish to thank Mr. Krish Krishnan, founder, Sixth Sense Advisors, Hoffman Estates, Illinois, USA, and Dr. Raja Roy Choudhury, Dean and Director, Prestige Group of Institutions, Indore, Madhya Pradesh, India, for contributing to this book. Their contribution is deeply appreciated.

The Great Transition

There has been tremendous progress in science and technology advancements in the past few decades, particularly in the last thirty-five years. What was a fantasy at one time is now a reality. Due to humans' significant progress, distances have shrunk, communication over great distances has become easy and fast, collection of vast data and compressing them in tiny spaces and gadgets are now possible. Besides, artificial intelligence is aiding and replacing human effort in many areas. These have become the order of the day. These technological breakthroughs have made life comfortable and opened new opportunities and markets. Intellectually, humankind has made significant progress. However, competition has also become sharper, and the pace of product and skills obsolescence has become much faster. The knowledge and skill required to succeed in this rapidly changing environment differ from prior periods. Education in more than one discipline may be required. It must be an amalgam of various fields of knowledge, mainly digital technology, its tools, and applications. Innovation and creative approaches are necessary for all areas. Today's businesses must operate, survive, and grow in this challenging environment. Smartly harnessing a person's intelligence, strength, innovative thinking, and skills is essential for overall peace and progress. It is of paramount importance to acquire new knowledge and skills and their application to the changing environment. If due recognition of this aspect is considered and action is initiated for course correction, it will positively affect the individual and the organization to which they belong.

Coping with Trends

One of the most significant developments in the past couple of decades has been the growth of globalization. However, "anti-globalization" sentiments are growing at the same time. The Brexit process saw the exit of the United Kingdom from the European Union. In the United States, the Trump Administration pulled out of the Trans-Pacific Partnership (TPP). It replaced the North American Free Trade Agreement (NAFTA) with the USMCA (United States, Mexico, and Canada Trade Agreement). The strained relationship between the United States and China and Russia's invasion of Ukraine has caused global supply chain disruptions of an unprecedented scale. The specter of inflation has gripped the United States forcing the U.S. Federal Reserve Bank to take aggressive steps to control it.

On the other hand, several major economies, including China, face the threat of recession. The headwinds of inflation and recession make the global economic scenario highly uncertain and rapidly evolving. Companies must operate and succeed in this complex and extremely challenging global business environment.

About fifteen to twenty years ago, the term "BRIC" was used to refer to Brazil, Russia, India, and China. Since then, Brazil and Russia have faltered. Due to the severe sanctions imposed by Western nations on Russia following the Ukraine invasion, its economy will likely face unprecedented economic pain for the foreseeable future. Even though the high oil prices have provided a short-term boost to the Russian economy, its long-term outlook is dismal. Russia finds itself increasingly isolated in the community of nations. China is also facing many challenges. The group that holds the highest potential for sustained economic growth is ICASA (India, China,

Africa, and Southeast Asia). However, each of these countries faces challenges. If these markets overcome their internal problems, they hold the potential for rapid and continued progress and expansion. Within ICASA, Africa has the highest potential. But it also has the most significant challenges. China's success on the global stage has shown that economic power creates geopolitical power. However, China faces a demographic disadvantage. The impact of its aging population and its disastrous one-child policy, which has severely skewed the sex ratio, are now being felt. Even though the one-child policy has now been abandoned, it will take at least a generation for the sex ratio to get rebalanced.

In addition, the COVID pandemic has had a severe deleterious impact on the Chinese economy. Therefore, its status as the flagship of the global economy is a moot point in the near future. One of the bright spots on the global stage is India. It has a large pool of skilled English-speaking workforce and enjoys the "demographic dividend." More than 50 percent of its population of 1.3 billion is under twenty-five. This fact will likely result in significant and sustained domestic demand for the foreseeable future. Its prowess in information technology and start-up culture, which has firmly established itself, portends a bright economic future for the country. This trend is facilitated by a business-friendly government that has launched many innovative programs to encourage entrepreneurship and economic growth. The government of India has also removed many colonial/socialist era laws and regulations that had shackled private-sector businesses and stymied economic growth. Given these favorable trends, India will likely replace China as the engine of global economic growth, at least for the near future. However, India does face some unique challenges, such as communal strife and tensions on its borders with China and Pakistan. In addition, the parliamentary elections scheduled in May 2024 is perhaps the most consequential elections in India since its independence from Britain in 1947. If it can overcome these daunting challenges, it can take its rightful place as an important player in the global arena.

One of the critical challenges of the future will be reducing resource consumption. Companies must adapt to operating in a resource-constrained environment. Advances in analytics, automation, and innovations in materials science, workspace designs, digital technology, Internet connectivity, and renewable energy sources enable resource consumption reduction. Technology is also having a significant impact on resource production, as well as reducing resource intensity. As technology progresses, revealing efficiency and opportunities across industries, companies should exert more influence on their cost structure. Given these developments, companies should be alert to resource-related business opportunities. For instance, composite materials, 3-D printing, and similar technologies have already transformed industries such as automobiles, aviation, electronics, and medicine. Therefore, companies should quickly seize opportunities that emerge or risk being pushed aside by their more agile competitors.

The pace of Industry disruption due to technological changes is accelerating. This disruption is causing the vital foundations of industry structure to change. Although this is widely viewed as an opposing force, it may also contain opportunities.

Technology is spurring competition that impinges on revenue and profit growth. But it is also creating new opportunities to improve corporate performance. Aligning a company's digital game plan with its corporate strategy has become a strategic imperative and a critical factor in differentiating between winners and losers. Corporate leaders with vision, sagacity, and foresight who can build an agile organization and keep up with the pace of change will have exceptional opportunities.

Even before the onset of the COVID-19 pandemic, the global business environment was very challenging. In such a situation, it is erroneous for a CEO to believe that a company's or industry's status quo will remain. The fundamental assumptions underlying the status quo must be identified and challenged. Besides, a concerted effort must be made to explore the possibility of turning an organization's limitations into strengths. When a company faces a challenge, it should carefully examine the experience of other companies facing similar problems and successfully resolve them.

If a company wants to disrupt an existing industry, it must, at the outset, identify the assumptions implicit in current strategies. Elon Musk cofounded PayPal. PayPal was a game-changer in the payments industry. In 2002, eBay acquired PayPal. This transaction resulted in a USD 175 million windfall for Musk. He has since parlayed this money into a diversified group of companies, including electric car company Tesla, space exploration company SpaceX, brain implant start-up Neuralink, tunnel construction company the Boring Company, a solar energy firm Solar City, and the messaging platform Twitter, now renamed X. These companies have attempted to disrupt their respective industries and have been quite successful.

Another example is that of Netflix, which transformed the video rental business by challenging the underlying assumptions. Blockbuster, which had a commanding market share in this industry once, did not challenge that business's assumptions. Consequently, it went out of business.

After identifying the assumptions, a company that wants to disrupt the industry must try to invalidate one or more of them. This strategy will enable the company to formulate a radically different business model that differentiates it from its competitors. Uber disrupted the cab industry with a fundamentally different ride-sharing model.

Companies can also succeed by combining products or services, or trends traditionally viewed separately. Many years ago, the founder of Sony, Mr. Akio Morita, noticed that young people were becoming increasingly mobile and loved music. Combining these two trends, he created one of the most successful electronic products ever—the Sony Walkman.

CEOs who wish to disrupt the industries they operate in should form groups with diverse expertise and experience. These groups should be mandated to explore new combinations of products and services. Furthermore, forming alliances with providers of complementary products must be examined as they are likely mutually beneficial.

The COVID-19 pandemic forced companies to operate in a resource-constrained environment. However, working in such a situation can also trigger creative strategies. Therefore, the CEO should actively encourage employees at all levels of the organization to develop innovative approaches.

Constraints can also be self-imposed and used as a tool to spur innovation. India's successful Mars Mission is an excellent example of frugal engineering caused by being forced to operate in a resource-constrained environment. Despite its meager budget, India's Mars Mission was a success on the very first attempt, a feat that no other country has been able to achieve to date. Another successful mission by the Indian Space Research Organization (ISRO) was the soft landing, for the very first time, of a spacecraft near the south pole of the Moon in August 2023. The total budget for this mission was less than the budget for many Hollywood movies! Instead of lamenting about the lack of funds, India's space scientists were able to successfully complete the missions through innovative strategies and resource optimization. Their success in this regard can provide valuable insights for companies.

Dare to Be Different

An aggressive attitudinal change and innovation in all aspects of managerial approach and action are required to be daringly different. Finding ways to do things better, break the monotony, and enhance curiosity while at work, with the enormous amount of knowledge, wisdom, and tools available now, will enable employees to gain new experiences. It is essential that learning must be integrated into all aspects of the business organization. Employees must feel comfortable making suggestions, taking risks, experimenting with new ideas, and giving and receiving free and frank feedback. Teamwork and a collaborative approach must be encouraged to produce better results. The pooling of cross-disciplinary expertise, wisdom, and skills is required. It must be developed for effective teamwork if people still need them. The chief executive must ultimately handle all feedback information—customer complaints, employees' grievances or aspirations, suggestions, and safety.

An important issue in this context is how an organization can elevate itself to the next level.

The areas that need particular focus for improving performance, value creation, and meeting the challenges of the competition are:

- Enhancing customer experience
- Digitization
- Mergers and Acquisitions and Corporate Restructuring
- Emotionally connecting with people
- Making an action plan and implementing it
- Pursuing a well-thought-out, carefully calibrated inorganic growth strategy. Organic growth is usually too slow in today's hyper-competitive business environment. Hence, an

acquisition-driven growth strategy becomes the preferred growth option and an essential tool for value creation.

- Reallocating and deploying resources to those business units that are performing well and reduce allocation to underperforming divisions.
- Judiciously investing in capital expenditure. Companies should seize the opportunity to buy mission-critical equipment at bargain prices during a business downturn. By doing this, they will be well-positioned to scale up operations when business picks up.
- Improving productivity. This task can be accomplished by restructuring business units, rationalizing locations, investing in automation, right-sizing the workforce, and terminating unprofitable business units. A company's goal should be to aspire to be at the top of its industry regarding productivity.
- Focusing on product differentiation. Customers are bewildered by a dizzying array of choices regarding products in today's business world. Therefore, differentiating its products from competitors becomes a strategic imperative for any company that dares to be different.

Like a game of cards, CEOs must play with the hand they are dealt with. However, the strategic choices made by a CEO early in their tenure will overcome the disadvantages of being granted a weak hand. Specifically, the CEO should leverage the benefits of artificial intelligence, digitization, cloud computing, and other emerging technologies to obtain a competitive advantage. In developing countries, there is tremendous pressure on land, resulting in high rental costs. Therefore, companies should explore creative ways of letting their employees work remotely. In addition, the CEO should ensure that the organizational units in the company do not operate in silos. There should be a seamless exchange of information between organizational units. This strategy will foster innovation and create value.

Digitization, a Vital Tool for Competitive Advantage

One of the most significant strategic dilemmas facing many companies is how to utilize, rather than get knocked down by digitization, an incredibly disruptive economic force.

Digitization, data analytics, and artificial intelligence are rapidly spreading across industries globally. They are changing the contours of the competitive landscape and profoundly impacting businesses. Adapting to these disruptive forces has become an organizational imperative. However, many corporate executives need to pay more attention to the growing momentum of digitization and the behavioral changes and technology propelling it. They often do not realize the scale of the tsunami of disruption caused by this unstoppable force. They will likely fade away unless companies adapt their business model to this powerful force. Firms that need to be faster to adopt digitization are likely to be attacked by agile and digital adversaries. These attacks can severely drain the revenues and profits of existing players in the industry. However, these incumbent players can contain the damage if they adopt an offensive corporate strategy that willingly cannibalizes existing businesses and aggressively redeploys resources to new digital platforms.

Many incumbent companies may be slow to respond aggressively to the changes in the competitive landscape caused by digitization, possibly because implementing robust digital strategies requires these players to overhaul their legacy IT systems, surmounting cultural and strategic constraints. Many companies are reluctant to disrupt their business model for an uncertain digital future. But this inaction may put their company at great peril.

Digital technologies can open new avenues to organic growth for companies with the capabilities, agility, and tenacity to take advantage of them. In this context, most companies fall into three categories: investors, creators, and performers. Investors squeeze funds from low-growth initiatives or unproductive costs to redeploy capital to promising initiatives. Creators build value by coming up with new products and services. Performers attempt to grow through a continuous process of optimizing core commercial capabilities.

Digital transformation requires a fundamental change in the way business is conducted. As companies embark on the digital transformation journey, they must remember how receptive the organization and its people are to this technological headwind. The CEO has a vital role in helping the organization cope with the challenges of digitization. The goal for a CEO should be to build an adaptive, agile organization that can quickly and effectively respond to challenges and opportunities as they arise. Being the first mover can confer a significant competitive advantage to a company. Early movers have a learning advantage. They can launch prototype products and refine results in real-time. Subsequent players who play catch-up will be behind on the competitive curve. In such an environment, industries are being transformed, and industry lines are blurring.

Therefore, more than developing strategies in the context of one's industry is required. Companies should consider the ecosystem as a whole rather than having a narrow focus on just their company/ industry. Successful companies around the world are expanding their ecosystems. They use artificial intelligence and other cutting-edge technology tools to create a very high level of customer service and, often, a personalized buying experience. Digitization permeates every aspect of the business, including products and distribution, business processes, supply chains, and ecosystems. The challenge for many companies is to devise ways to digitize their existing businesses while creating innovative new business models that will enable them to respond quickly to changing customer requirements. It has become a necessity to make an appropriate investment in digitization. A digital reinvention must deliver the competencies required to meet an organization's strategic goals. As it is unlikely that any organization will have all the skills internally, it must develop an ecosystem of external partners with specific industry expertise and capabilities. Bold and seamlessly integrated digitization strategies will be the biggest differentiator between organizations that succeed and those that don't. The most significant rewards will follow those organizations that create digital disruptions. A robust organizational culture enhances the ability of a company to perceive digital threats as well as opportunities, strengthens the actions that companies can take in response to the challenges of digitization, and bolsters the coordinated execution of these actions across functions, departments, and business units within the company.

Furthermore, the breakthrough in digital technology has opened new horizons of approaches and opportunities. Besides, it has opened many possibilities in artificial intelligence, 3D printing, data analytics, cloud computing, and interactive portable devices. Studying these trends will help businesses shape their strategies to navigate the winds of change and quickly adjust themselves to improve performance and enhance their value. Society's progress is due to some intelligent thinkers daring to do things differently and boldly. The technological advances during the past few decades have changed the nature of work and employment.

The landscape of functional business knowledge is rapidly evolving. Perennially popular topics such as strategy and organization are clashing in unforeseen ways with the forces of digitization, big data, analytics, and artificial intelligence. Those clashes are spawning new business opportunities and require new organizational capabilities. These dynamic changes are undoubtedly causing disruptions to employment and how businesses are operated for stability and growth. Therefore, lifelong learning has become a strategic imperative today. In the future, people will have to use cognitive skills more. Many people will need various competencies to stay "afloat" in the increasingly complex and hyper-competitive global business environment. Training them to use these tools to enhance decision-making and gain a competitive advantage will be a significant challenge. The management must emphasize the importance of continuous learning at all levels of the organization. This emphasis will enable workers, managers, and senior executives to use technology appropriately and to interpret information intelligently to improve the organization's results, health, and well-being. The future of learning now is not in a classroom. It is learning while working. Employees can act more quickly, and usually more effectively if capabilities bubble from within and education is personalized for individuals. Fortunately, people analytics tools enable organizations to manage and develop their people more precisely than ever.

Data and Competitive Advantage

Many corporate executives believe they can gain an unassailable competitive advantage by harnessing customer-centric data. They think that the more data they collect and process, the better it is. However, the fact is that such executives tend to overestimate the benefit gained through data.

Compiling customer information and using it to make superior products and services is not recent. It has been around for a long time. But the process was constrained by the technology available at that time. It was also expensive and time intensive. The emergence of cloud computing and other new technologies has dramatically reduced the time required to process and interpret vast amounts of data. Customization of a company's products and services to an extent never thought possible before is now possible with the help of machine learning.

Assessing whether the competitive edge provided by data-enabled learning is sustainable is important. The first question in this regard is the incremental value added by customer data. Another question is how fast the marginal value of data-enabled learning tapers off. In other words, how quickly does the incremental benefit cease to be beneficial? If the incremental benefit from customer data remains significant even after a sizable customer base has been acquired, then the product and services will have a significant competitive advantage.

If the data becomes obsolete fast, it will enable a rival to quickly enter the market because that rival does not need to use its competitor's knowledge gleaned from the data over many years.

A company will be conferred a competitive advantage if the customer data is proprietary and cannot be purchased from external sources. However, technological advances can blunt this advantage. Therefore, a company needs to invest resources in research to enhance its technology and keep its rivals at bay.

The benefits gleaned from proprietary data can dissipate if rivals can replicate these benefits without similar data. But if the improvements in products or services are hidden in a complicated production process, it would make it difficult for rivals to replicate them. In addition, if the insights gained from customer data mining change quickly, it would make it more challenging for competitors to imitate. If the data from one customer improve the product for other customers, it would be a critical advantage in competing for new customers.

The faster the insights gained from the user data are incorporated into the products, the more difficult it would be for rivals to catch up. Speed is the key in this context.

If customers believe that the learning from data mining gets incorporated fast into the company's products, they will be interested in knowing how many people are adopting the product.

The belief that one needs many customers to obtain the benefits of data mining is a fallacy. Most of the learning from customer data can be attained with a relatively low number of customers. The mantra should be to extract the maximum value from the minimum number of customers. In some cases, AI could make the value of data-enabled learning redundant. Data-enabled knowledge can enhance and personalize product offerings if used judiciously. However, the competitive advantage from data-enabled learning is possible only when the value added by customer data is significant and long-lasting. If the data is proprietary and not easily replicable, it will lead to product enhancements that are not easy to replicate. In the future, enhancing product offerings using customer data will become a strategic imperative and a vital prerequisite for success.

Innovation Strategy

Several companies invest a great deal of resources into their innovation strategy. But yet, the benefits of this strategy still need to be discovered. Many of these initiatives, undertaken with good faith, fail to generate the expected results. Alternatively, these innovation initiatives peter off after some time. Companies need help to sustain the momentum. Why? While the failure to execute the strategy may be a significant factor in this regard, other factors are also responsible for the lack of sustainability of these initiatives. An important factor is the need for a coherent innovation strategy. Another factor is the failure to align innovation initiatives with corporate strategies. Without a carefully thought out and planned innovation strategy, the innovation initiatives might become a collection of disparate best practices. While pursuing these best practices is commendable, they may not go well with each other. They may exist in separate silos. Due to this reason, the expected benefits may still need to be realized. Each independent strategy will involve trade-offs. With an innovation strategy, an organization can make trade-off decisions and create an innovation ecosystem to generate the desired results.

There is no "one size fits all" regarding innovation strategy. What has worked well for one company may not work for another. Therefore, copying and implementing a company's innovation strategy and implementing it without customizing it to the organization's specific needs will not be prudent. A company should design its innovation system considering its competitive needs and value-creating objectives. In the absence of an umbrella corporate innovation strategy, different parts of the company may end up pursuing conflicting priorities. The management should seamlessly integrate a company's innovation strategy with its business strategy and value proposition to generate the desired results. With such integration, a company's innovation initiatives are likely to succeed.

For an innovation strategy to be successful, it must achieve broad societal benefits and create value. The management must maintain a razor-sharp focus on these objectives. It must also be willing to commit the necessary resources. Strategy formulation that is not backed by adequate resources will be an exercise in futility. Companies need to recognize and prepare for the fact that their value-creating innovations will attract competitors. The actions of these competitors will put downward pressure on prices and erode margins. But by constant process innovation and creating an ecosystem of reliable suppliers, a company can ward off its competitors. To maintain its dominance, a company must develop complementary products and services to lessen customers' chances of switching to rival brands. Apple has done this very successfully.

Innovation should not be considered a one-time exercise. It must be a constant process. Otherwise, agile and nimble competitors will likely dominate and grab market share.

If we dig a little deeper, we realize that there are different types of innovation. A company should adopt the innovation strategy that is best suited for its value-creating objectives. The standard innovation strategy does not require altering a company's business model. Instead, it builds on a company's core competencies and meshes with its existing business strategy. Disruptive innovation refers to a radically different business model that shakes up an industry and challenges conventional assumptions regarding that business. Revolutionary innovation refers to a strategy that is based on a technological breakthrough. This strategy requires significant investment in R & D. A company that wishes to pursue this strategy requires some very profitable products that will generate the cash flow needed to fund the R & D. Hybrid innovation strategy is based on a blend of technological advances and changes in the existing business model. It is based on the premise that this blend will trigger innovations that will give the company a continued competitive advantage.

There is sometimes a tendency to discard standard innovations in favor of fancier types of innovation. But the undeniable fact is that many companies, such as Microsoft and Apple, have used the traditional innovation strategy to generate billions of dollars of profit. This fact does not imply that companies should concentrate solely on standard innovations. On the contrary, companies should carefully examine the various innovation options available to them and choose the option that will be best suited for their value-creating objectives and give them a sustained competitive advantage. A blended approach to innovation initiatives is likely to generate the best results.

In the context of the blended approach, a question is what percentage of resources should be allocated to the various innovation approaches the company decides to pursue. That decision is a judgment call that the management has to make and will be based on a host of unique company-specific actors. The resource allocation decision will be a crucial factor in determining the success or failure of the company's overall innovation strategy.

The technological landscape is rapidly changing, and a company cannot afford to rest on its laurels even if its innovation strategy is successful. It has to constantly scan the business environment and quickly latch on to emerging tailwinds. This strategy will enable it to continue to grow and be profitable, despite the vicissitudes of the global business environment. The onus is on the top management to decide the best innovation strategy for their company and implement it. They must also be prepared to modify the strategy if business conditions change. A dynamic innovation process is essential for the continued growth of the organization.

Disruptive Innovation

Disruptive innovation is a term that has been used a lot lately but which needs to be better understood. Many people use this term to mean the entry of an upstart company into an established industry which causes the companies already existing in that industry to be adversely impacted. But this definition of this term needs to be narrower and more specific. Each situation is different, and to paint all industries with a broad brush in this regard would be erroneous.

In the past, it was challenging for a small company to take on big companies in an industry. But the rapid technological advances in recent years have enabled an upstart company to compete effectively against its established rivals. Traditionally, the big companies in an industry have focused on the most profitable segment, namely, the high-end segment. They have invested their resources in catering to the exacting demands of their high-end customers. In doing so, they must pay more attention to the market's low-end, less profitable segment. As the late Dr. C. K. Prahalad pointed out in his seminal work, "The Fortune at the Bottom of the Pyramid," with the right strategy, catering to the needs of the low-end segment of a market can be very profitable too. There are numerous examples of companies, especially in Asian countries such as India, which have become very profitable by meeting the needs of the low-end segment of a market through innovative packaging and marketing strategies.

By leveraging technology, small, upstart companies have established a foothold in established industries by focusing on the low-end segment of the market. Then these companies move upstream and meet the needs of the mainstream part of the market.

Aided by technology, they offer convenience, flexibility, and very competitive pricing for their products and services. This strategy enables them to gain acceptance in the mainstream segment of the market and gain volume. This strategy disrupts that industry. Big companies blindsided by the disruption caused by their smaller but more nimble and agile rivals falter and start going downhill. Once the forces of disruption set in, an industry can't return to the pre-disruption days.

Disruptive innovations occur in two ways. In some industries, an upstart company disrupts the industry by focusing on the low-end segment of the market and offering a low-priced, good-quality product. For instance, a local detergent brand, "Nirma," became very successful in India by providing good quality, low-priced detergent powder. A relentless advertising campaign aided this. This strategy helped Nirma compete against multinationals, such as Unilever, that focused on high-end customers. Unilever's products were unaffordable for India's growing middle-class consumers. There are numerous examples of companies similar to Nirma, especially in the Asian context, that have disrupted their respective industries.

The other way disruption occurs is when innovative companies create a market where none existed. These companies create a want or need among consumers for products and services that did not exist in the past. The key here is to carefully observe the changing needs of consumers and develop products quickly that will satisfy those needs.

These are the two ways in which disruptive innovations occur. The critical point to note in this context is that mainstream customers will adopt the products a disruptor offers only if they perceive those products to be of good quality. Product acceptance will happen only when mainstream consumers are satisfied with the quality of the products and the price. But once that acceptance sets in, sales volume will multiply. This fact will drive down the price in that market and make the established players scramble to catch up with their agile and nimble competitors.

Using the term "Disruptive Innovation" is erroneous to refer to a product or service at a specific time. Using this term to refer to an evolved product or service is more appropriate. In other words, disruptive innovation is a process, not a one-time event.

One key question in this context is why established companies tend to get blindsided by their agile and nimble disruptive competitors. The mean reason is that the process of disruption takes time. Disruptors gradually established a foothold in the low-end segment of the market, improved their quality, and aggressively priced their products or services to attract mainstream consumers. Due to their small size, these companies are not viewed as a threat by the big companies. It is too late when the big companies realize that the small companies are a severe threat to them. This fact makes the big companies scramble to respond effectively to their agile and nimble rivals. Another factor behind the success of the disruptors is that their business models are very different from that of the big companies in the industry, who tend to have traditional business models.

It is important to note that companies should not become overzealous and ditch their still profitable business models because disruption is happening in their industry. They should focus on innovation, improvement in quality, and better customer service in their core market to ensure continued profitability while creating a new division to respond to the disruption in their industry. The disruptive business can be kept as a stand-alone, separate from the core business. While this approach would be preferred, companies that adopt this strategy must be prepared for the fact that the disruptive business can draw customers away from the core business. In other words, the cannibalization of customers by the disruptive business may occur.

When a small company tries to disrupt an industry, the established companies may choose to fight back with all the means at their disposal. They may enhance their innovations and offer better products and services at competitive prices. Their size and financial strength may help them to drive down the price point to a level that the small company will not be able to match. The big companies may either push their small competitors out of business or acquire them to strengthen their product portfolio. We need to recognize that the entry of a small company into an industry intending to cause a disruption does not necessarily imply that the demise of the big companies is impending.

That said, it is unfortunate that some big companies commit resources only to their existing profitable businesses. However, the writing on the wall indicates that disruption is starting to happen in the industry. Companies may have a division focusing on potential opportunities arising from the ongoing disruption. Unless the management is willing to commit resources to that division, it is unlikely to create an impact.

In summary, disruptive innovation can happen in any industry in any country. Therefore, it is critically important for established companies to constantly scan the business environment and identify trends that can cause disruption. Once these trends have been identified, these companies must formulate and implement quickly an effective strategy to respond to these trends and establish a "first mover" advantage. Failure to do so may result in them being knocked off the pedestal that they have occupied for many years by agile, nimble rivals.

Purpose-Driven Strategy

A company's goals in any country are to attract and keep talent, meet customers' needs, and conduct business in a manner that satisfies the community and the regulators and earns an attractive rate of return on invested capital.

Articulating its purpose is an important business decision for any company and must be anchored in strategy. Business leaders must have a clear and cogent understanding of how their corporate purpose extends beyond their brands' and advertising objectives. Corporate purpose is about the core of a company. Its goal is to garner support from various stakeholders and enrich their lives. Successful companies define their purpose and build their company around that purpose. Clearly articulating its corporate purpose enables a company to demonstrate how it can meet the requirements of all its stakeholders. Corporate strategy should be centered around purpose and must have the unequivocal backing from the top management, augmented by adequate financial support. If properly planned and executed, this strategy can result in profitable growth leading to sustained value creation. It would also enhance ties with all the stakeholders of the organization.

Focusing on purpose can help a company expand its market, creating more opportunities. High-growth companies follow this formula. These purpose-driven companies can expand their ecosystem by identifying growth opportunities and quickly establishing a dominant presence in these growth areas.

Of course, executing this strategy successfully requires new core competencies and a nimble and agile organizational structure. The odds of this strategy succeeding are dramatically enhanced if it is centered around the organization's core purpose.

Given the vicissitudes of global business and the ferocity of competition, companies that lack a purpose-driven strategy will likely be pushed aside by their nimbler rivals. Under pressure and facing strong headwinds, these companies may improve their value proposition by modifying their products, services, or business models. However, the gains accrued through this strategy are likely to be short-term. On the other hand, a purpose-driven strategy would enable a paradigm shift in doing business, resulting in sustained growth, revenue generation, and value creation.

Companies that follow a purpose-driven strategy identify and commit themselves to value propositions that allow them to enhance their relationship with their customers. This approach, in turn, would create additional revenue streams and profits. Visionary companies are adept at spotting customers' unmet needs by leveraging technology and quickly developing solutions to address those needs. These companies' primary goal is to improve their customers' quality of life.

Companies that follow a purpose-driven strategy either take the retrospective or prospective approach. Companies that follow the former path build on the company's past and change the organizational structure, corporate culture, and business model to meet competitive challenges. In a sense, it is an evaluation of history to prepare the roadmap for the future. Companies that follow the latter approach look ahead and redefine the ecosystem in which they want to operate. They aim to identify future trends likely to impact their business and prepare the organization to take advantage of them.

Clearly defining the corporate purpose helps a company to get the word out on what it stands for. It provides a blueprint for action and can be a source of motivation for all the employees of the company. However, more than merely having a purpose is required. It must be backed up by action. Otherwise, the company is likely to lose credibility.

What is a purpose statement?

1. It lays out a long-term goal for the company.
2. It gives the goal an idealistic sheen by affirming that the company is committed to fulfilling its social responsibilities.
3. It communicates the company's mission.

But not all companies "walk the talk" regarding purpose. Some companies have a purpose-driven statement but act on the stated purpose only in superficial ways. However, some companies can be called Deep Purpose Organizations. These companies are committed to both positive societal and commercial outcomes. Their decisions, actions, and processes are undertaken with the corporate purpose in mind. At the same time, they do not let their idealism affect their business goals and objectives. Purpose gives these organizations a constant source of clarity in decision-making. They approach each choice with the determination to serve all stakeholders to the maximum extent possible while recognizing that, sometimes, trade-offs are unavoidable.

For it to be effective, a purpose-driven strategy must permeate all levels of the organization to be successful. It should not be a concept only at the upper echelons of management. More than merely engaging in Corporate Social Responsibilities (CSR) is required. The corporate purpose must be integrated into the core business of an organization. It must permeate into every aspect of the business. Only then will it give the desired results.

It is challenging to transform a profit-maximizing system into a purpose-driven one. But it is a fallacy to think that implementing a purpose-driven strategy at a publicly traded company is exceedingly difficult. With proper planning and seamless execution, it can be successfully implemented in publicly traded companies. Effective communication with all stakeholders in this regard is critical. If the stock market starts seeing the beneficial effects of this strategy, it is likely to reward the company by boosting its stock price.

The first step in drafting a corporate purpose is establishing a core team of representatives from all the vital internal constituencies. This approach will give the feeling of collective responsibility for formulating and implementing this strategy.

Corporate purpose can have various focus areas. A competence-focused purpose provides a clear value proposition for customers and employees. A culture-focused purpose fosters internal alignment and collaboration with important partners. A cause-focused purpose links together customers, employees, and communities. At the core of these linkages are the societal benefits that the company creates.

While drafting the corporate purpose, it is essential to examine how it will enhance a company's value proposition to customers and provide a distinct competitive advantage.

A carefully and thoughtfully drafted statement of purpose can help a company achieve the following:

1. Enhance consumers' preference for its products and services.
2. Improve the connection that employees feel to the company and each other.
3. Build the company's reputation as an excellent corporate citizen.
4. Increase opportunities for profitable growth while reducing business risk.

However, corporate purpose can achieve its objectives only when it matches a company's value proposition and meets the aspirations of both internal and external stakeholders. The critical test of a company's purpose is whether it improves how it operates.

The prudent approach to enable purpose to enhance corporate value is to allocate people, time, technology, and money to purposeful causes designed to create long-term sustained benefits for as many stakeholders as possible.

In summary, a purpose-driven strategy makes good business sense, motivates stakeholders, and benefits society. Companies that adopt this path are likely to experience sustained value creation.

Strategy and Creativity

If the top management wants the executives to develop pathbreaking strategies, it must provide them with the resources to enhance creativity and the freedom to implement their ideas. There are different paths to successful strategy formulation. One path is to identify the traditional assumptions regarding the company's industry. The next task is to examine whether any of these conventional assumptions could be proved false and evaluate the benefit of doing so. Challenging traditional assumptions could lead to a breakthrough and disrupt an industry.

Combining things traditionally viewed as separate can be leveraged to create a new, profitable revenue stream. An effort must be made to determine whether a company can combine complementary products and services. Companies from different industries can join for mutual benefit. The partnership between Nike and Apple and Nest and Amazon has clearly shown that combining their respective offerings can create new customer value and profit for the partner companies. There is a trend toward more interaction between humans and machines, with machines taking over low-level tasks, leaving humans to focus on more creative activities.

The top management must create groups of executives from diverse backgrounds and charge these groups with exploring new combinations of products and services that would be profitable for the company. These groups should also be empowered to reach out to providers of complimentary products and services to determine whether such companies would be willing to combine forces for mutual benefit.

A sagacious strategist may not view an organization's weaknesses as limitations but instead, focus on how to turn those weaknesses into strengths. It may be possible to turn these so-called weaknesses or limitations into strengths through creative thinking. The top management could deliberately impose some constraints to force executives to discover new ways of thinking and doing. Innovative solutions may emerge when people are forced to operate in a resource-constrained environment. India's successful Mars Mission is a prime example of success despite being forced to operate in a resource-constrained environment.

When faced with a problem, an executive could try to determine how a similar situation was solved in a different context. This approach may bring forth valuable insights. Executives could also explain their business to their friends/acquaintances from another industry. Those friends/acquaintances may look at the company from a different perspective. Valuable insights may emerge from this interaction.

Strategy Execution

A company can achieve a prime position in the competitive landscape through its strategy, product offerings, and technology. But its ability to stay in that position depends on its execution ability. Many companies that are good at strategy formulation and planning fall short in execution. Execution is the process of converting plans into actions. One of the strategies companies use to improve efficiencies is to redraw the organizational chart. However, mere reorganization of the organizational chart is likely to yield short-term benefits only. Lasting change can happen only when strategy execution is rigorously followed.

When profit margins come under pressure, most companies opt for restructuring. Layers of management are removed, and massive layoffs are seen as a panacea for declining profitability. This strategy does yield some short-term benefits. But the long-term effects, especially regarding massive layoffs, can be deleterious. In their zeal to cut costs, the management often destroys the organization's DNA. Employee morale is shattered. In addition, in order for these changes to be effective, they must address how decisions are made in the organization and who is accountable for making those decisions. Managers need to have clarity on their roles and responsibilities to establish accountability. Besides, without clarity on roles and responsibilities, managers will not be clear about what decisions they need to make and by what time. In addition, the lack of a strong link between performance and rewards will demotivate managers and affect productivity. Therefore, companies that wish to improve performance through enhanced execution should first establish clarity on roles and responsibilities. Then, managers should be held accountable for the actions that they are expected to do. Thirdly, there should be a clear link between performance and rewards. This link will act as a powerful motivator and enhance productivity. Managers should also stay in positions long enough to see the outcome of their launch initiatives. They should also be held accountable for their actions. The results can form part of their performance reviews.

There are some common traits that companies that are known for their organizational effectiveness share:

1. Employees clearly understand their roles and what they will be held accountable for. There is clarity regarding roles and responsibilities in such organizations.
2. Divisional and geographic area leaders are given explicit performance targets to meet. But they are also given control over spending.
3. Managers at the front lines quickly convey to the top management the changes they discern in the competitive landscape. This strategy helps the top management to strategize and adapt to those changes quickly.
4. Pricing is based, not on cost, but on market realities.
5. Operational responsibility is delegated to managers on the front lines. Top management is focused mainly on global strategic issues.
6. Silos are dismantled. Business units are urged to collaborate. Cocreation is encouraged and fostered in a nurturing and enabling environment.
7. The planning process is inclusive.
8. Each business unit is made responsible for its P & L statement.
9. Business units are allowed to make design, manufacturing, and pricing decisions on their own.
10. Decentralized decision-making gives business units greater control over market decisions.

11. Information flows horizontally across different business units without any impediments.

12. Top management gives great importance to customer-outreach programs and constantly endeavors to know the pulse of the customers.

In summary, strategy execution is a **critical key to value creation**.

Organizational Capabilities

There should be recognition of the importance of organizational capabilities. These capabilities are critical determinants of the success and failure of an organization. A company cannot build these capabilities in a short time frame. They are acquired through many years of judicious investment by the top management in key human resource areas. It takes vision and foresight to make these investments. Merely investing in resources will not ensure organizational success. It has to be matched by investment in people with the required skills and training to produce the desired results. Eventually, these capabilities are what a company becomes known for. These capabilities are also the basis for the perceptions in the minds of the customers toward the company as well as its products and services.

Competitors can usually copy a company's product portfolio strategy or technology. But it is much more difficult for them to copy a company's capabilities. In addition, once an organization becomes known for its capabilities, it inspires confidence in the minds of investors about the financial soundness of the company and its future earnings. Market capitalization is primarily based not on current earnings but on perceptions of future performance. Therefore, investing in building capabilities ultimately results in value creation.

The starting point for building capabilities is to attract and retain talent in the organization. A company can attract talent by offering attractive compensation and a conducive work environment that facilitates professional advancement and personal growth. In addition, a company should also invest resources in enhancing the skills of its existing employees to ensure that its personnel have the requisite skill set to deliver outstanding results. A company can also gain access to talent through strategic alliances and partnerships. The management should also constantly devise ways to retain the talented employees it has attracted. In addition, to avoid gaining a bloated workforce, a company should also weed out poor performers. The continued presence of such people in the organization is likely to have a deleterious effect on other employees.

Given the frenetic pace of changes in the global business environment, speed of execution becomes a critical determinant of success. It is a crucial capability that companies should build. Recognizing promising opportunities is not sufficient. The ability to quickly act on them and establish a competitive advantage becomes critical. The shorter the time frame between the concept and commercialization of ideas, the better it would be from a value creation perspective.

Creating a positive perception of a company and its products/ services is crucial. Brand identity becomes **a key determinant of profitability**. This identity can be built by judicious investment in marketing and advertising. In addition to a company's external image, its internal image is also vital. If the employees have a positive image of a company, it will be a source of pride and motivation. This fact will translate into greater productivity because when employees feel proud of their company, they will be motivated to do their best for the organization.

A company should clearly articulate its goals and convey to the employees that they would be held accountable for their performance. Establishing accountability, therefore, becomes a critical organizational capability. Accountability also helps to enhance employee performance because they know that failure to meet the pre-determined goals would have consequences. The employees would also know that meeting or exceeding targets would be rewarded.

Successful companies encourage and facilitate collaboration across business units. Collaboration can not only result in cost savings but can also lead to the co-creation of innovative products and services. An effective tracking system can also be implemented to track and measure collaboration across business units. Therefore, fostering collaboration within the organization becomes a key organizational capability.

Organizational learning is also an essential organizational capability. Benchmarking, experimentation, and continuous improvement are vital elements of organizational learning. A conducive corporate environment is needed for these elements to flourish and for learning to happen.

Another crucial organizational capability is the ability to produce leaders who will collectively move the company to the next level of performance. Successful companies have systems that will identify future leaders and nurture them into influential leaders who will add significant value to the organization.

Well-managed companies are skilled at building trust and long-term relationships with their most important customers. Since a large proportion of profits come from these customers, these companies go to great lengths to establish connectivity with them. This process involves these customers in critical human resources functions and exposes the company's employees to these elite customers.

Another characteristic of organizational capability is the ability of the top management in a company to articulate its corporate strategy clearly. This approach enables the employees to imbibe the strategic vision and internalize it. Successful companies also focus on innovation from a multi-faceted perspective. The goal is to enthuse employees, please customers, and enhance the trust and confidence of the investors. These companies also excel in controlling costs and constantly focusing on efficiency improvements.

In summary, organizational capabilities are essential to corporate success and value creation. A capabilities audit will be beneficial in this regard. It will help evaluate the company's intangible assets and identify the areas in which it needs to build capabilities that would give it a competitive advantage and lead to value creation.

Learning from Failure

In the business world, failure is sometimes inevitable. Learning from failure is of critical importance. Most organizations state that they are committed to it. Usually, a team is constituted to analyze what went wrong; a report is generated and shared with several employee groups. But the efforts to learn from the failure fade away after some time. Therefore, lasting change does not occur. Gleaning insights from failures is more challenging than it seems. It is a complex process that has to be formulated carefully for maximum benefit. It must be more than just a superficial exercise, devoid of a firm commitment to imbibe and implement the lessons learned. There is a tendency in many organizations to assign blame for failure instead of trying to understand the underlying reasons for the failure.

A company that has created a culture where employees can admit and report failures without fear of retribution must ensure that this culture is not misconstrued as condoning poor performance. Executives often need help to balance their desire to create an open work environment and maintain high levels of performance and productivity.

Understanding the underlying causes of failure will avoid the blame game and help formulate an effective strategy to learn from failure. Failure can result from many causes. Sometimes, an employee may deliberately choose to violate corporate policies and processes. Secondly, an employee may deviate from the prescribed specifications accidentally. Thirdly, failure may result from deficiencies in the process even though the employee may be competent. Fourthly, failure may result from the task assigned being too challenging to accomplish within the time frame allowed with the resources that have been provided. Fifthly, the process designed for a task may be too complex. Sixthly, there may be a lack of clarity about the way forward, resulting in erroneous decision-making by the employee.

Appropriate training and support are essential to avoid deviation from processes. The use of checklists may also be beneficial in this regard. If deviations do occur, they must be quickly identified, and appropriate remedial action must be taken. A system of continuous learning must be implemented. Corrective action must be taken when deviations occur. The feedback from this experience must be incorporated into the learning process so that it does not happen again.

Most fields of work are inherently uncertain. Many organizational failures would be attributed to this uncertainty. The complete absence of failure may be a utopian goal. Despite the best efforts, minor deviations or shortcomings may still occur. But serious failures can be prevented by formulating and implementing best practices in safety and risk management areas. It is important to note, however, that small failures that go unnoticed can build up to become much bigger failures. Therefore, prompt corrective action is essential.

Some companies conduct experiments by launching small projects in areas different from the company's existing business lines. By carefully analyzing the outcome of these projects, the management decides whether to commit resources to these new business areas. Formal public announcement of these new ventures happens after the management is reasonably confident of the success of these initiatives. Even if some of these projects fail, the learnings would benefit the management and help them reformulate their strategy.

Visionary leadership is essential to create a corporate culture that fosters trust and encourages employees to identify failures and take prompt corrective action. A corporate culture in which finding fault with someone is its core tenet is harmful and could cause a breakdown of trust. It will also create a sense of alienation among employees. This process will ultimately lead to value destruction.

The first step to course correction is detecting failures, especially smaller ones that may lie hidden. The management must create an environment conducive to detecting such failures before they mushroom into much larger failures. Unfortunately, in many organizations, employees hesitate to report failures due to fear of the negative ramifications of such reporting on their job. Therefore, the stigma of reporting failures should be removed. Employees should be encouraged to speak up without fear of retribution.

After a failure has been noticed, it is essential to delve deep into the bottom of the problem. Every failure will offer insights that will be very useful in the future. It may also be fruitful to experiment with failure. Each experiment is an opportunity to gain additional insights. As Henry Ford, the doyen of the automobile industry said in 1905, "Failure is only the opportunity to begin again more intelligently."

In summary, failure is inevitable in any organization. But ignoring it and not learning from it can be fatal.

Developing Resilience

The COVID pandemic blindsided many companies around the world. They lacked the tools and strategies to cope with this unprecedented challenge. This lack of preparedness led to the demise of many businesses. Therefore, insulating the company from sudden, unexpected shocks has now become a strategic imperative. Companies must build resilience—the ability to cope with unforeseen challenges and emerge successfully.

Companies need to come to terms with the fact that unexpected events will become more common in the future. Climate change, geopolitical vagaries, and frenetic advances in digital technology will likely fuel these events. The digital revolution has unleashed an unprecedented level of connectivity. It has also resulted in a dramatic increase in the availability of data and the speed at which data is processed.

The climate change conundrum has forced companies to make sustainability a central part of their corporate strategy. Consumers are paying increasing attention to sustainability practices at companies. Therefore, it would be prudent for companies to embrace the 17 Sustainable Development Goals put forth by the United Nations (https://sdgs.un.org/goals) and develop an action plan to attain as many of these goals as possible. Having sustainability woven into the corporate credo is not just an altruistic exercise. It also makes good business sense. Companies that delay embracing sustainability as a core corporate goal will risk being pushed aside by their nimble competitors.

Given the rapidly changing global business environment, companies need to shed their myopic focus on short-term performance, develop the ability to withstand unexpected threats, and come out stronger from any crisis. In other words, companies need to be **resilient**.

Some CEOs think that it will suffice if a company is financially resilient. But more is needed. Climate change is a looming and growing threat. It can affect the sourcing, production, and distribution of goods and services. It can cause severe disruption to the global supply chain. This threat will cause production costs to go up sharply. Companies are also likely to be under increasing pressure from various stakeholders to develop strategies to cope with climate change. Only a resilient company will be able to withstand such pressures.

The word "resilience" has different connotations. It encompasses a range of areas such as financial, operations, technology, organization, reputation, and business model.

Regarding financial resilience, companies must maintain adequate liquidity to cope with revenue decrease, sudden cost spike, or credit-related matters. Sufficient liquidity will also help a company deal with the loss of market share and capital-raising constraints.

Regarding operational resilience, companies need to have the production capacity that will enable them to adjust to the vagaries of demand without compromising on quality. In addition, given that supply chains can be suddenly disrupted, it is crucial to plan for such contingencies so that providing goods and services to customers is not adversely impacted.

Regarding technological resilience, companies must build a strong, secure, and flexible infrastructure to prevent cyber security threats. Technologically resilient companies also use robust data to achieve organizational goals while complying with privacy and regulatory requirements. Such companies also have a robust business continuity and disaster recovery plan in place so that customer service and business operations are not impeded.

Companies must align their words and actions with their core values regarding reputational resilience. In today's business environment, where the spread of information is very rapid, companies are held accountable by a wide range of stakeholders. Companies should clearly articulate their mission, values, and purpose as the blueprint for corporate actions. Regular communication with stakeholders, managing their expectations, and responding to criticism promptly and transparently is very important.

Regarding business model resilience, companies must maintain flexible business models that can quickly adapt to changes in demand, technology, and regulations. An organization must be agile and nimble to adapt to changes in the competitive landscape rapidly.

As outlined above, these various dimensions of organizational resilience should be embedded into the corporate strategic plan. In addition, companies must make a serious effort to anticipate challenges/disruptions they are likely to face and plan to cope with them even before they materialize. It is a fact that a company's management is unlikely to be able to anticipate all challenges/disruptions. Therefore, quickly reacting and taking effective actions when unanticipated challenges/disruptions appear will be crucial to corporate success. Decisive action at the right time can prevent the loss of shareholder value.

A good starting point would be for a company to conduct an "organizational resilience audit." This audit will not only provide information on the current situation regarding resilience but will also identify critically deficient areas that must be addressed on a priority basis. This process will also help a company to develop a resilience roadmap that can serve as a blueprint for the future.

Shareholder Value Creation

Creating shareholder value is considered the "holy grail" regarding management objectives. During the past few decades, it has become part of management parlance. The relentless pursuit of shareholder value creation and the short-term focus this strategy entails is often touted as the cause of the ills ailing Corporate America. After the stock market collapse in 2001, many controls were implemented in the United States. These measures included passing the landmark Sarbanes Oxley Act (SOX) in the United States in 2002. Unfortunately, the short-term focus has persisted, especially among American firms. However, if we step back and look at this issue objectively, we realize that it is long-term value maximization that is the key. So, what is the roadmap for maximizing long-term value?

It has become fashionable for companies to manage earnings. Companies deliberately lower earnings guidance so that it becomes easier to beat the consensus earnings forecast based on the guidance. Companies then indulge in various gimmicks to meet or exceed the consensus earnings forecast. Reducing spending on research, development, and maintenance can cause value destruction in the long run. Eventually, companies find themselves unable to meet the expectations of investors. This trend leads to the demise of the company.

Strategic corporate decisions must be undertaken, considering the impact of these decisions on cash flow generation and long-term value creation. They should not be undertaken based on their likely impact on quarterly earnings. If the company has a menu of strategic choices, it should choose the one with the greatest value-creation potential. A scenario/sensitivity analysis should be conducted to determine how sensitive this value is to the vicissitudes of the competitive landscape and the regulatory environment and the underlying assumptions made in the forecasting process.

Concerning resource allocation decisions, those operating units with the most significant value creation potential should receive the bulk of the funds. Restructuring options should be explored for those operating units with limited value creation potential.

Companies should carefully pursue mergers and acquisition (M&A) decisions because a bad deal can destroy corporate value faster than anything else. It is erroneous to base M&A decisions on EPS accretion or dilution. The decision regarding M&A deals should be based on their strategic value-creation potential. It is also advisable to be highly conservative when forecasting synergies and put a post-merger integration plan in place even before the deal is concluded. In addition, acquiring companies should avoid getting afflicted with the "Winner's Curse Syndrome."

Companies should continually scan the business opportunities to see if any potential buyers out there who would be willing to pay a significant premium over the company's estimated cash flows and pay an attractive price for its other assets, such as real estate and brands.

In the past, companies used to take pride in doing everything themselves. In today's hyper-competitive global business environment, companies should focus on the activities that add the greatest value and where they have a significant competitive advantage. They should outsource activities that other companies can perform at a lower cost. In other words, a razor-sharp focus on those activities that generate the "biggest bang for the buck" will facilitate value creation.

In some companies, the management likes to hoard cash. Whatever the reason for hoarding cash, it is a fact that there is a huge opportunity cost of holding excess cash reserves. The right thing to do is to return the money to the shareholders through dividends and share buybacks. Returning excess cash to the shareholders also reduces the possibility that the management may use that cash to make erroneous, value-destructive decisions. A share buyback with the sole purpose of boosting EPS should be avoided. A buyback should be considered only when it makes economic and strategic sense.

How the compensation packages for senior executives are structured can also influence value creation. In companies committed to value creation, stock options for senior executives are structured in a manner that will give them an incentive to work toward long-term value creation. Stock options are a good way of incentivizing senior executives because they are required to focus on overall corporate performance. Stock options do not work well as an incentive for managers of operating units. Therefore, other methods of incentivizing managers of operating units, such as Shareholder Value Added (SVA), should be explored. Stock options and other incentives should be prudently designed, after taking into consideration the nature of the executives' work, to create long-term value. Performance should be evaluated over at least three years. This approach will ensure that the focus is on long-term performance.

A company can also develop quantifiable indicators of value. Middle-level managers can be incentivized by evaluating their performance on key value drivers that they directly impact and reward them accordingly. General and vague financial indicators will not be suitable.

To avoid the tendency of many executives to take short-term measures to boost the company's stock price and then cash out their stock options, a company may have a requirement that top executives' own stock at least equivalent to five times their base salary. However, we need to recognize that such conditions will harm the liquidity and diversification objectives of the top management.

An antidote to the myopic short-term earnings focus is to offer relevant information that impacts value creation. This strategy will reduce uncertainty among investors and build trust in the management's decisions and actions.

These principles, if applied judiciously, will enhance long-term value creation.

ESG Initiatives and Value Creation

Much debate has been about whether ESG (Environmental, Social, and Governance) initiatives are worth the investment. These questions become louder when a company faces a paucity of resources, such as during a recession, or is blindsided by an unforeseen event, such as a pandemic. But the fact is that ESG initiatives become even more critical during an event such as a global pandemic or an economic downturn because it makes the company more resilient and gives it strength to cope with such events.

It is also a fact that perception drives behavior in the stock market. Companies seen as good corporate citizens who care about society are perceived more favorably than companies driven solely by profit. DEI (Diversity, Equity, and Inclusion) have recently been very important in the Corporate world. Companies that invest resources in meaningful DEI initiatives that make a real impact are often rewarded by the stock market.

Many companies engage in a bunch of ESG activities primarily based on advice from consultants and often driven by the actions of competitors. However, ESG initiatives should not be mere random activities. They must be embedded in strategy and built into the very fabric of the company. They must also be enmeshed into operations. This approach will generate accurate results, and the stock market will reward these efforts. Sustainability, social responsibility, and excellent governance practices are three pillars that will confer a competitive advantage to the company and lead to value creation. However, for ESG initiatives to succeed, the top management must be fully committed to them and willing to invest the resources necessary to help them succeed.

Some people argue that companies must engage in ESG initiatives because a company is part of society and draws its sustenance from society. Therefore, it has obligations toward society. But rather than looking at ESG strictly from a moral perspective, it must be understood that ESG initiatives also make perfect business sense. ESG activities motivate employees and increase their productivity. It also creates a favorable perception in the customers' minds and builds trust. This strategy is likely to translate into increased sales. There may be other potential benefits too. A company that gains a reputation for its ESG activities can raise capital at a lower cost. This will in turn enhance value creation. This strategy may also attract investors who wish to invest in companies that perform well from the perspective of ESG.

There is also a growing trend worldwide, especially in the European Union and several emerging markets, requiring companies to be more transparent concerning their ESG disclosures. Activist shareholders also demand that companies commit to more ESG investments and hold them accountable if they fail. For example, in many countries, regulations require more gender diversity on corporate boards. ESG practices are increasingly becoming an essential and integral part of long-term corporate strategy.

Before delving deep into ESG initiatives, it is essential for a company to clearly define its corporate purpose, and then create a culture built around it. Then, ESG practices with the most societal impact must be identified and embedded into long-term corporate strategy. A company's ESG practices must distinguish it from its rivals and be difficult to imitate. An accountability structure needs to be created. The management should determine the operational changes required for the smooth implementation of the ESG strategy. To make the whole process successful, transparency is essential. It is also important to build trust with investors. This approach will ensure that the ESG initiatives will lead to long-term value creation.

The board is crucial in ensuring that ESG initiatives are embedded in corporate strategy and are correctly implemented. The strategy must be linked with purpose. Investors value companies that can clearly articulate their corporate purpose. In addition, for ESG initiatives to succeed, a conducive corporate culture is essential. The employees should believe that the ESG initiatives suit their company and themselves. The board and the company's top management are pivotal in making this happen. The board should also have the strategic vision and capabilities to ensure the company maintains excellent ESG performance.

Previously, companies thought they had to choose between sustainability and profits. But now, sustainability and ESG initiatives are vital to building trust among investors and creating long-term value for the company. It would be helpful to appoint a senior executive as a chief sustainability officer with a mandate to coordinate all ESG issues at the company and make course corrections as needed.

In summary, companies that do not invest resources in sustainability and ESG initiatives will be at a competitive disadvantage. Therefore, embedding purpose into strategy and building a culture around this has become a strategic imperative.

Focusing on Growth

One of the characteristics of the last ten to twelve years is the easy availability of low-cost capital. This fact, coupled with modest economic growth in the Western world, resulted in a sharp drop in the cost of equity capital. There was a reduction in the after-tax cost of debt as well. The abundance of capital re-ignited the Profitability versus Growth debate. When the cost of capital is high, it is prudent for a company to focus on improving profitability. In such a scenario, margin improvement should be the primary focus due to the core principle of the Time Value of Money, which states that a dollar today is worth more than a dollar to be received in the future. But when the cost of capital is low, focusing on growth would create more value for a company. When a company's ROE is well above its cost of equity capital, strategies that enhance growth should be pursued.

Companies have resorted to strategies to improve margins when capital costs are high. However, focusing on growth is more beneficial in a low-cost capital environment. That said, the nature of the industry also influences the growth versus profitability conundrum.

Most companies in the Western world are obsessed with improving their margins. So, they resort to cost-cutting by laying off thousands of employees. Sometimes, these job cuts destroy a company's DNA. Therefore, no matter how deep the cuts, it does not result in sustained improvement in margins. Companies also try other cost-cutting measures, such as corporate restructuring and offshoring.

Why is there such an obsession with improving margins and not focusing on growth? The main reason is that growth requires new ideas. There is a dearth of ideas in many companies. Many companies' management struggles to develop growth options to propel their company to the next level. Apple is an exception. Its iPhone business has elevated the company to a whole new level. It has spawned an ecosystem of app developers, resulting in the iPhone becoming the most sought-after mobile phone in the world.

Many companies have a risk-averse mentality. They actively discourage risk-taking and are generally hesitant to experiment with new ideas. They favor cost-cutting and squeezing out more profitability from a firm's operations. They need to realize that cost-cutting will work only up to a point. There should also be a focus on top-line growth. This is a critical necessity.

The paucity of new growth ideas has made companies pause and consider options for spurring growth. There is a belated realization that conditions conducive to innovation must be created to stimulate growth. Some companies give their employees greater autonomy and authority to bring new ideas to fruition. In addition, they allow executives to conduct experiments and provide incentives for risk-taking. These companies realize that taking advantage of low-cost, abundant capital is a strategic imperative. Unfortunately, some great ideas aren't implemented and are stuck in bureaucratic bottlenecks. Only a few ideas to spur growth get implemented. In many companies, there is a risk-averse mindset when making strategic investments. While this attitude may be appropriate when capital is scarce and costly, it is certainly not advisable when capital is cheap and abundant. Sticking to options perceived as "safe bets" and being unwilling to take risks is not prudent. Once the "focusing on growth is risky" mindset permeates the organization, it would be challenging to change it. Some companies have been able to change this mindset. For example, Google regularly places bets on risky new ventures unrelated to its core business. But the management does not give a blank check to those managing these new ventures. When the new ventures are not panning out, the management quickly pulls the plug, and terminates them.

In summary, when capital is abundant, companies that arise to create value should focus on growth. The impediments to growth must be identified and removed. Creative ideas put forth by employees must be encouraged and rewarded. The skills and capabilities of the employees must be carefully nurtured and enhanced. The companies must be willing to place bold bets and commit the resources necessary for these bets to fructify. The industry's nature must be considered when deciding which growth ideas to pursue.

When Growth Stops and Revenue Diminishes

A successful company may become complacent and may overlook the emerging threat from smaller, nimble, and agile competitors. Suddenly, the management may be blindsided by a sharp fall in revenue. When this happens, the management tends to blame external factors such as the state of the economy, government policies, and regulations. This strategy is designed to deflect blame from the management to outside forces. But the reasons for stalling revenue must be addressed by the management.

Many big companies like to position themselves in the market's premium segment due to their attractive margins. They become entrenched in that segment and believe in the effectiveness of their business model. But by doing so, they cannot effectively counter the actions of their smaller, nimbler, and agile rivals who may offer a better value proposition for the customers. This approach could lead to first stalling in the revenue and then a precipitous drop in revenue. Then, the realization dawns on the management that urgent changes are needed. But at that stage, the management's actions are too late. The company cedes ground rapidly to its smaller rivals. Eventually, this leads to the demise of the company. The main reason for the end is the failure to respond quickly and effectively to the changes in the competitive landscape. It is also a fallacy for these companies to believe that their investment in building their brands over many years would be sufficient to cope with the vagaries of the marketplace. Brands are essential and do give a competitive advantage to a company. However, observing the changes in the market and adapting to those changes quickly and effectively is even more critical. In contrast, the new entrants into the industry have a keen sense of what the consumer wants and modify their product offerings to cater to those needs.

Sometimes, a successful company becomes a victim of its success. The management develops an air of nonchalance and becomes indifferent to the changes in the competitive landscape. The management of such companies treats their smaller rivals with disdain and doesn't perceive them as a severe threat. But this proves to be a very costly blunder as they start losing market share to their smaller rivals and industry disruptors. The loss of market share starts gradually and then picks up pace as competitors encroach more and more into the big company's business segments.

Another reason for growth stalling and revenue falling is the faltering of innovation in the organization. The breakdown of innovation in the organization negatively impinges on updating existing products and services in accordance with the consumer's changing needs. This results in the loss of market share to rivals who are more agile and nimble. Market share, once lost, is very difficult to regain. If the breakdown of innovation in an organization leads to systemic inefficiencies, it can cause serious repercussions. There can also be the risk of misallocating R&D resources to projects that promise quick returns. This risk can adversely affect long-term projects. Regarding R and D spending, it is not the total amount that matters, but how that money is allocated.

Companies sometimes decide that their core business is saturated. This belief leads to the erroneous view that their core business has no growth opportunities. So, they prematurely abandon their core business without identifying and exploiting growth opportunities that may still exist in their core business. This strategy is another reason for stalling of revenue. Exiting the core business also opens the door for smaller and more agile firms which quickly capitalize on the opportunities in the space that has just been vacated by the company that prematurely exited its core business.

Companies that have relentlessly pursued process improvements and operational efficiencies in their core business have widened the revenue gap between themselves and their rivals in the same business.

Strategy execution in any organization requires skilled and committed executives with a razor-sharp focus on the goals that must be achieved. If there are lacunae in the top management ranks, strategy execution efforts will be adversely impacted. Without capable people in key roles with the requisite skills and experience, revenue is likely to stall.

Some companies have a strict promote-from-within culture. While it is true that such a policy builds loyalty toward the organization, it can also hinder the company's ability to respond quickly to changes in the competitive landscape. The absence of executives with the skills and experience to effectively respond to emerging business challenges and heightened competition could play a key role in slowing growth and revenue staling.

It is also essential that the top management ranks should consist of executives with diverse backgrounds so that the top management is well equipped to meet emerging challenges successfully. Suppose the top management team consists of executives with similar skill sets. In that case, they may not have the breadth of skills and experience needed to compete with new, agile, and nimble competitors and quickly respond to rapid changes happening in the marketplace.

There is often a disconnect between a company's corporate strategy and the changes happening in the external environment. Failure to address this problem promptly can be fatal. Often, the beliefs and assumptions that have driven a company's growth become enshrined in the company's DNA. As a result, decision-making in the company becomes sclerotic. Revenue growth stalls and the company starts sliding down toward oblivion. Therefore, it is incumbent upon the management to create a conducive environment in the top management echelons so that executives can articulate viewpoints that diverge from that of the CEO without fear of recrimination and retribution. Deeply ingrained assumptions need to be questioned and modified as required.

While growth can stall despite the management's best efforts due to unforeseen changes in the external environment, the chances of it happening can be significantly reduced by taking the appropriate measures internally and anchoring the decision-making process firmly on the company's strategic value creation objectives. In addition, it may be beneficial to charge teams within the organization to develop competing visions of the company's future and the path forward. This process, if conducted in a conducive environment, can help executives to come to a consensus on the strategy to put the company on a firm path toward revenue growth and enhancement in profitability, despite the vicissitudes of the business environment.

The Internet of Things (IoT)— Continuum of Opportunities

(The authors thank Mr. Krish Krishnan, Founder, Sixth Sense Advisors, Hoffman Estates, Illinois, U.S.A., for contributing this article).

The future is here and looking at us in the eye. We are now in a world where our personal and professional lives are more digital than ever.

Businesses' big question is whether they are ready for the onslaught of data in terms of volumes, velocity, and variety. Questions that follow are: do they know how they will secure the right data segments and how they will manage it? Who can and will govern the data over a period? And do they know what backup strategies will be needed for this infrastructure to evolve with resilience? These are all questions for categorizing and strategizing the *Internet of Things* (IoT).

Focus on Data

The foundational step for the Internet of Things is an evolving machine learning model and artificial intelligence mixed into algorithms for managing and monitoring systems, users, and applications. Several entities that make up the Internet of Things are:

- Algorithms
- Artificial intelligence
- Data Analytics
- Data Architecture

- Data formats
- Data lifecycle
- Governance models
- Machine-to-machine conversations
- Platforms: cloud and mobile
- Security

The questions we plan to ask in the future also bring a perspective on skills. The millennial generation is the next generation of the workforce. They are a Google-and-collaboration-based group of innovators and thinkers. This characterization means that we need to create a platform that is not focused on technology but focused on data for those of us who are innovating the future today.

These opportunities open a world of new frontiers and innovation that is extremely exciting, and a lot of this *newness* exists in terms of platforms and possibilities. As we investigate the new world enabled by data, the algorithms we can execute in this realm are all here, and more are being examined. They are all very flexible and not mathematical, and they have started creating an effect on the world somehow, shape, and form.

Interconnectedness

Today, the programming world is drawn into designing and developing solutions to create and enable value for the end consumer in an instant. We see emerging technologies with scalability, security, and support as mandated by data requirements. For example, think about the interconnected things in our lives today. We can control our home heating, cooling, and lighting from remote applications. This capability is fed with information on the everyday usage of power and resources from our smart thermostats and grid meters.

Device-based connectivity and conversations are driven by data transmitted between all devices, including encryption, transmission, and decision support. Another example is the electric cars that several manufacturers sell today. These automobiles come with rechargeable batteries. Moreover, the batteries can start drawing a charge from nearby charging stations indicating how long the charging will take. The repeat charges can be transmitted to the manufacturer with encrypted vehicle identification numbers (VINs) and battery numbers for statistical and mathematical purposes.

Another example is the rising use of personal, wearable health devices provided by vendors such as Android, Apple, Fitbit, and Nike. People can wear these devices when exercising and during everyday activities such as walking, sleeping, and eating. These devices upload statistics based on your profile, age, and fitness and health goals to your smartphone, tablet, and laptop for you to use and update.

As we can see, we continuously generate a lot of data. All of this is shared with the producers of these products based on their requirements for further usage. The new world is digital and will have more data from all areas, including some examples discussed here. The challenges are collecting the data, sorting through the noise and acquiring the signal in a streaming process, and then collecting the entire set of signals for algorithmic analysis on a time-period basis in a twenty-four-hour cycle.

The future vision offers a glimpse of the ongoing changes driven by the Internet of Things (IoT). This article looks at how enterprises are evolving around the Internet of Things and some of the important considerations that come with those changes.

From the enterprise perspective, the Internet of Things is defined as everything connected in a digital universe. The core of this definition is that the availability of the application or thing and its data is in a connectable ecosystem, which today is a given expectation of any platform.

A few critical pieces of architecture need to be considered in this ecosystem for these reasons:

- *Bandwidth constraints:* Not all areas of the world are "smart" yet.
- *Reliability:* Constant availability of infrastructure helps ensure the reliable processing of data.
- *Infrastructure resources:* Unless you are ready for cloud-driven infrastructure, which is digital transformation, there are limitations on the availability of infrastructure to process data on a continuum.
- *Extremely high, scalable networks:* A serious uplift is needed for the mobile infrastructure, but are you already implementing the most current infrastructure? And can it handle multichannel levels of usage?
- *Security:* This component is the key to the castle—is it ready?
- *Privacy:* We have moved into a new realm of data, security, privacy, and protection. Are you ready with the latest privacy options, and have you implemented them?

These considerations have become the critical set of underlying requirements to implement a successful digital transformation program that can lead to an internet of things-ready enterprise. Consider some examples.

Mobile medical devices

In today's world, medical devices patients use in hospitals and at home or work can transmit data on demand. From a data security and privacy protection perspective, this on-demand data transmission is good because of data availability and usefulness in proactive patient health management. However, it can be harmful because the information can be hacked or incorrectly shared.

How does one address this problem? How can you prove to an audit and compliance team that this kind of data transmission is being guarded as an asset? And how can this protection still allow the use of the digital world data to derive the insights that can provide a foundation for improving machine learning, algorithms and models, visualization, and interactive treatment in remote healthcare services situations?

In many hospitals today, the bed and all the associated equipment have radio-frequency identification (RFID) that makes them digital-ready. Even the patient chart, which becomes digital following EHR regulations in the United States, is expected to go digital. This digitization makes it easier to manage patients and comfort their families.

Digital medical devices raise other issues around data regulations and their format, the protection of assets, issuing data to the patient at the time of services and after hospitalization, readmittance regulations, and state and federal laws. As we develop the technology frontier in healthcare, several products and solutions that help address these considerations are available from vendors such as GE, Motorola, Siemens, and other mobile device vendors. Along with the front end, several changes are being adopted in the back end through big data technologies, data security algorithms, machine learning, and other software implementations.

And in parallel with these changes, vendors such as Predixion have been working to bring analytics in visualization to the forefront. This effort helps manage key performance indicators (KPIs) across the spectrum. Into this mix of data and technologies, we can implement an IBM Watson solution that provides an integrated stack of data and search analytics to improve how we use this data. The emergence of these technologies, interfaces, and data requires that we strategize a solution architecture that enables digital transformation.

Smart buses

We are moving toward automation of information from all aspects of life, including smart cities, transportation, and more. Today's fundamental transformation is the connected bus, a program Cisco and the San Francisco Transportation Department piloted. The innovation underlying this concept is integrating and using information and communications technology to allow knowledge, people, traffic, and energy to flow efficiently. Increased efficiency enhances how people experience urban life, streamlines the management of cities, and reduces the urban environmental footprint.

As a part of this program, which was tested in 2009 and has been incrementally improved, the Connected Public Transit incorporated various smart-traveler features that use real-time information to provide dynamic—changeable—guidance based on user profiles and context. This functionality is the key feature of an Internet of Things application, which creates powerful insights and outcomes. By implementing this system, the overall carbon footprint of the city of San Francisco was reduced as people began enjoying the feature-rich and user-friendly transportation system. Today, this hallmark case study has become a globally implementable platform that can enhance safety for women, children, and senior citizens in many countries worldwide. The smart bus demonstrates a compelling use case and implementation of the Internet of Things and how simple solutions can influence society.

Internet of Things technology continues to grow at a fascinating pace, and increasing opportunities to innovate in an Internet of Things world proliferate. The skill and technology layers needed to make the Internet of Things a reality for today's world start with machine learning, deep learning, graph databases, and real-time data management. And they continue with advanced analytics, sensor data frameworks, infrastructure platforms such as Apache Hadoop, NoSQL, and programming languages such as C++, Go, Java, and Python.

The most recent wins in this new land of opportunity are the National Institutes of Health's (NIH) Precision Medicine Initiative (PMI), fraud analytics in healthcare, and financial analytics with advanced clustering and classification techniques on mobile infrastructure. More opportunities exist in space exploration, smart cars and trucks, and new forays into energy research. And remember the intelligent wearable devices and devices for pet monitoring, remote communications, healthcare monitoring, sports training, and many other innovations.

Five Steps to Innovation

How do we achieve success in this journey and become innovative always? What are the critical success factors? What are the risks? The processing of Internet of Things data requires a step-by-step approach that is evolutionary:

- Acquire data from all sources. These sources include automobiles, machines, mobile devices, networks, sensors, wearable devices, and anything that produces data.

- Ingest all the acquired data into a data swamp. The key to the ingestion process is to tag the source of the data.

Streaming data that needs to be ingested can be processed as streaming data and saved as files. Ingestion also includes sensor and machine data.

- Discover data and perform initial analysis. This process requires tagging and classifying the data based on its source, attributes, significance, and need for analytics and visualization.

- Create a data lake after data discovery is complete. This process involves extracting the data from the swamp, enriching it with metadata, semantic data, and taxonomy, and adding more quality to it as feasible. This data is then ready to be used for operational analytics.

- Create data hubs for analytics. This step can enrich the data with master data and other reference data, creating an ecosystem to integrate this data into the database, enterprise data warehouse, and analytical systems. The data at this stage is ready for deep analytics and visualization.

The key to note here is that the last three steps are all empowered in creating data lineage, data readiness with enrichment at each stage, and a data availability index for usage. This strategy must be implemented, and here is where Google, Amazon, and Facebook showed more prowess, as their primary use was around search.

Critical factors for success

While the steps for processing data are similar to what we do in the world of big data, the data here can be big, small, wide, fat, or thin and can be ingested and qualified for usage. Several critical success factors can result from this journey:

Data: You need to acquire, ingest, collect, discover, analyze, and implement analytics on the data. This data needs to be defined and governed across the process. And it would help if you handle more volume, velocity, variety, formats, availability, and ambiguity problems with data.

Business goals: The most critical success factor is defining business goals. Without the right goals, the data is neither helpful nor are the analytics and outcomes from the data valuable.

Sponsors: Executive sponsorship is needed for the new age of innovation to be successful. If no sponsorship is available, then the analytical outcomes, the lineage and linking of data, and the associated dashboards are all not happening and will be a pipe dream.

Subject matter experts: The people and teams who are experts in the subject matter must be involved in the Internet of Things journey; they are critical to the success of the data analytics and using that analysis.

Sensor data analytics: A new dimension of analytics is sensor data analytics. Sensor data is continuous and constantly streaming. It can be generated from an Apple iWatch, Samsung smartphone, Apple iPad, a smart wearable device, a BMW 1 series, Tesla, or a hybrid car. How do we monetize this data? The answer is by implementing the appropriate sensor analytics programs. These programs require a team of subject and analytics experts to come together in a data science team approach to meet the challenges and provide directions to the outcomes in the Internet of Things world. This move has started in many organizations but lacks focus and requires a chief analytics officer or chief data officer to make it work.

Machine intelligence: This success factor refers to an ecosystem of analytics and actions built on system outcomes from machines. These machines work 24/7/365 and can process data in a continuum, which requires a series of algorithms, processes, code, analytics, action-driven outcomes, and no human interference. For more than twenty-five years the work in this area, has led to developments such as IBM Watson; TensorFlow, an open-source library for numeric computation; Bayesian networks; hidden Markov model (HMM) algorithms; and Decision Theory and Utility Theory models of web 3.0 processing. This field advances artificial intelligence algorithms and has more research and advancement published by Apache Software Foundation, Google, IBM, and many universities.

Graph databases: In the Internet of Things world, graph databases represent the most valuable data processing infrastructure. This infrastructure exists because machines and people will continuously stream and process data. It requires processing nodes across infrastructure and algorithms with data captured, ingested, processed, and analyzed. Graph databases can scale up and out in these situations and can process with in-memory architectures such as Apache Spark, which provides a good platform for this new set of requirements.

Algorithms: The algorithm success factor holds the keys to the castle in the Internet of Things world. Several algorithms are available and can be implemented across all layers of this ecosystem.

Risks and pitfalls

No success is possible without identifying associated risks and pitfalls. In the world driven by the Internet of Things, the dangers and pitfalls are all similar to those we need to handle daily in the world of data. The key is that data volume can cause problems created by excessive growth and formats.

Lack of data

A vital area to avoid within the risks and pitfalls is a lack of data, which does not identify the necessary data in this world driven by the Internet of Things architecture. This pitfall can lead to disaster right from the start. Be sure to define and identify the data to collect and analyze, its governance and stewardship, its outcomes and processing—it's a big pitfall to avoid.

Lack of governance

Data lacking governance can kill a program. No governance means no implementation, no necessary rigor to succeed, and no goals to be measured and monitored. Governance is a must for the program to succeed in the Internet of Things world.

Lack of business goals

No key business actions or outcomes can happen when no business goals are established. Defining business goals can provide clear direction on which data and analytics need to be derived with the Internet of Things data and platforms. Two essential requirements for these goals help avoid this important pitfall: executive sponsorship and involvement and the other is governance. Do not enter this realm of innovative thinking and analytics without business goals.

Lack of analytics

No analytics can lead to total failure and facilitates non-adoption and a loss of interest in the Internet of Things program. Business users must participate in the program and define all the key analytics and business applications. This set of analytics and applications can be documented in a roadmap and delivered in an implementation plan. A lack of analytics needs to be avoided in all programs related to the Internet of Things.

Lack of algorithms

No algorithms can create no results and translate to the non-adoption of the program. A few hundred algorithms can be implemented across the Internet of Things platforms and data. These algorithms must be understood and defined for implementation, which requires some focus and talent in the organization, both from a leadership and a team perspective. Algorithms are expected to evolve and need to be defined in the roadmap.

Incorrect applications

The use of incorrect applications tends to occur from business users who lack an understanding of the data on the Internet of Things platform, and it is a pitfall to avoid early on. The correct applications can be defined as proof-of-value exercises and executed to provide clarity. Proof of value is a cost-effective solution architecture build-out and scalability for the Internet of Things platform.

Failure to govern

If no effective data governance team is in place, implementing, or attempting any data or analytics, can be highly challenging. This subject has been a sore point to be resolved in all aspects of data but has not been implemented successfully very often. For any success in the Internet of Things, the failure to govern pitfalls needs to be avoided with an experienced and robust data governance team in place.

Fearing the unknown from data access

Why is the fear of the unknown a factor in the Internet of Things data? To answer this question, consider a few examples of using the Internet of Things today.

Smart thermostats

The arrival of smart thermostats represents a fascinating and powerful Internet of Things technology. For example, based on your choices for controlling temperature, lighting, and timing inside your home, you can use your smartphone or tablet to control these home environment conditions from anywhere in the world.

This capability has created much excitement in the consumer market. Millions of homes now have these devices installed. But what about the data part of this solution? The device needs to be permanently connected to the Internet to accommodate access and, more importantly, continuously send information to the power company, device manufacturer, or both. Hence, the fear of the unknown: imagine what can happen next if anybody can access these devices and obtain your credentials from the data stream.

Not only is identifying user preferences possible, but someone hacking into the smart thermostat can monitor your presence in the home, break in when you're not there, or worse. Once someone has access to the network, data theft can lead to other kinds of damage.

Is this solution that insecure? The answer is no. But ongoing work in data governance and data privacy attempts to address the security gaps that can cause concern. To minimize these concerns, the underlying security of the data needs to be professionally managed.

Smart cars

Electric automobiles manufactured by Tesla Motors and Nissan, for example, are touted for being purely electrically driven thanks to the amount of computerization and logistics that make driving them easy. Similar smart car development efforts are underway with the Google driverless car experiments, testing, and research at BMW, Mercedes Benz, and other auto manufacturers. All these smart car technologies are fantastic and thought-provoking. Still, smart cars can continuously communicate information—the vehicle's condition and geographic coordinates of its location—to the manufacturer and possibly the dealer where the vehicle was purchased.

This capability can induce worry—more so over whether the transmission data is hack-proof than whether the transmission is mechanically safe. And this concern is for a good reason. If a transmission is intercepted, actions such as passing incorrect algorithms to the engine that may increase speed or cause a breakdown or an accident in a driverless vehicle are within the realm of possibility. Hacking into a smart car can also result in other disruptions, such as changing the navigation system's map views.

This fear of the unknown from innovative car technology tends to be more with driverless cars than electric cars. Nevertheless, how can hacking smart cars be avoided? No regulations for this data and its security exist in the auto industry, and unfortunately, rules are being created after the fact.

Smart health monitoring

Remote monitoring of patients has become a new and advanced form of healthcare management. This solution benefits hospitals and healthcare providers and creates additional data management and privacy regulators. Monitored patients wear a smart device connected to the Internet to transmit data to a hospital, healthcare provider, or third-party organization that provides data collection and on-call services for the hospital or provider.

Although the data collected by an innovative, wearable device generally isn't specific to any single patient, enough data from these devices can be hacked, for example, to obtain credentials for logging into the network. And once a rogue login compromises the network, consequences can be disastrous. For now, the situation with remote monitoring of patients is reasonably well controlled. Still, security needs to be enhanced and upgraded for future implementations as the number of patients requiring remote monitoring increases. As demonstrated in the previous examples, electronic health record data requires improved management and governance.

Enhancing Customer Experience

Enhancing customer experience to gain a competitive advantage has become a new mantra for many companies. They wish to deepen their ties with their customers. This approach is a "win-win situation" for both companies and customers. Companies enhance their operational efficiencies, lower costs, and boost profits and customers get what they want quickly and seamlessly.

Building business and brand loyalty is essential for a sustained business relationship that will benefit a company and its customers. This strategy is the core objective of a company's efforts to enhance the customer experience.

Companies around the world spend millions to create brand awareness and loyalty. They also go to great lengths to provide an enhanced and seamless customer experience. The amount spent on such activities is an investment. Brand loyalty and improved customer experience will help a company achieve its value-creating objectives.

The ongoing digital revolution, which has been decreasing transactional costs, has recently picked up the pace with massive increases in electronic data, the pervasiveness of mobile interfaces, and the rising power of artificial intelligence. Combined, these forces are changing customer expectations and allowing almost every sector with a distribution component to reshape its boundaries faster than previously experienced.

In the near future, a growing number of industries will converge under highly customer-centric digital ecosystems. These ecosystems will encompass diverse firms that provide digitally accessed, multi-industry solutions. The relationship between these firms in the digital ecosystem will be commercial and contractual. These ecosystem relationships are enabling companies to meet increasingly exacting customer expectations.

The competitive landscape is rapidly changing. As boundaries between industry sectors continue to disappear, many CEOs of companies generating substantial revenue within traditional industry boundaries will be confronted by companies and industries that they never previously imagined to be their competitors. This new, rapidly changing environment will require the CEOs to have a different mindset and will need their companies to gain new competencies quickly. Defending a company's position will become critical. In this context, enhancing customer experience will be paramount and at the core of a company's value-creating objectives.

When silos characterize an organization, responses to rapidly changing customer needs are usually too narrow, with vital signs missed or acted upon too slowly, simply because they were seen in some other part of the company. These silos can negatively affect a company's growth and its value-creating ability. Therefore, a CEO must inspire the employees and convey a shared sense of direction. They should send the message across the entire organization that having a customer-centric approach and providing customers with a seamless, positive experience is vital for creating value.

Companies are realizing the increasing importance of customer-centricity and that consumers expect a seamless user experience. Companies that do not have secure customer connections risk being pushed aside by their aggressive data-driven competitors. Therefore, companies need to build and maintain emotional relationships with customers. They should use data to customize offerings, content to capture customers' attention, and digital engagement models to create a seamless customer experience. Also, they must launch initiatives to help keep and expand their customer base.

The digital era is forcing companies to get close to their customers and giving them the means to do so. The demands of customers have become exacting. This pressure is moving companies to devise innovative ways to meet those demands. A customer-centric organizational culture has become a strategic imperative. Instead of trying to guess what the customer needs while designing products and services, many companies are now making real-time adjustments to the features of their products and services based on their customers' direct input. This approach results in higher customer satisfaction.

Harnessing management skills and developing a robust and agile organizational structure, proper HR management, vision, leadership, and goals are necessary. However, all organizations should strive to enhance customer experience and create value for stakeholders. Doing so will enable the company to create value for the shareholders. Therefore, improving customer experience is critically important in any organization. A customer-centric approach is essential in this regard. Customer-centricity means being deeply entrenched in customers' needs, not just thinking about developing new products with additional features. It means reaching out to customers and developing products and services to help them become more competitive. Trust must be built with customers so that they feel that the company is a partner in their progress, growth, and success. Companies must demonstrate to customers that their requirements would be well understood and that they have the requisite facilities, technology, systems, skilled labor force, and other resources to enhance their confidence levels.

Companies should also demonstrate to customers that they can maintain uninterrupted supplies, consistency in quality, and adjust to volume changes and delivery times as needed. The customers should realize that the suppliers are a part of their progress and growth and cooperate to minimize their difficulties adjusting to their calls. There should be openness in the dealings between the vendor and the buyer. Any design or material specifications or quality parameter changes made or intended must be shared with the supplier well in time to meet the new paradigms without hurting both parties. They must work together for rapid growth, and progress should be clearly understood. The customers must feel that the company has sound systems and procedures and process checklists in place. These will build transparency, trust, and confidence and enhance the customer experience.

While the goal is to provide an enhanced customer experience for all customers, special attention must be paid to the most critical customers based on the account value. The formation of core groups to address the most valuable customers' needs in a timely and efficient manner is essential. These core groups should report directly to the CEO. When these customers know that the CEO is personally involved and is committed to providing them with an enhanced customer experience, they will be more inclined to build a long-term business relationship that will be mutually beneficial.

If enhanced customer experience is everyone's responsibility, then data on service levels should be available. Still, the CEO's responsibility is to decide which product lines to invest in and which ones to eliminate. They should have privileged access to the information needed to make those critical strategic decisions.

Leading companies are beginning to understand that they are in the customer-experience business and that how an organization delivers for customers is as essential as what it offers.

It takes patience to train employees to see the world from the customer's perspective and to redesign organizational functions to create value in a customer-centric way. The CEO should consider the customer, not the organization, as the center of this process.

It is a fact that customers' requirements have become more exacting. Satisfying customer demands poses challenges for any company as technology has enabled customers to make comparison shopping quickly and easily. Enhancing customer experience has become **a vital tool for value creation**.

Forming a holistic view of the complete end-to-end customer experience is essential. Such a picture will help the management understand the customer's entire journey. Too often, companies focus only on certain aspects of a customer's journey instead of taking a comprehensive view of the whole trip. A customer may be satisfied with a specific element of the journey with the company but may be disappointed with the overall experience. This disappointment could prompt the customer to consider alternate providers. In today's hyper-competitive business environment, lost market share is very difficult to regain. Therefore, retaining customers is of paramount importance. Positive customer experience is the critical element in keeping customers.

Focusing on the entire journey will please the customer and make it more likely that they will recommend the products/services offered by the company. Potential customers will be inclined to try a product or service if they have been recommended by someone they know and trust.

Articulating the corporate statement of purpose will likely create a distinctive customer experience. This statement of intent must be broken down into easy-to-understand principles or standards so that every employee assimilates them and acts accordingly.

Often, the decision to buy a product or a service is based on the customer's perception. Therefore, changing or shaping a customer's perception will generate significant value for a company. Besides, giving customers a feeling of control over the decision-making process can be very beneficial.

Effectively managing the entire customer journey is very important because even one bad experience can deter the customer from doing business with the company again. Agile digital companies are effectively leveraging technology to provide an enhanced customer experience. Their less nimble competitors must quickly adopt such strategies. Otherwise, they run the risk of becoming roadkill.

Companies that wish to provide enhanced customer experience will have to transform themselves. The organizational structure may have to be modified. Sophisticated data analytics techniques must be used to understand customers' needs better. The frontline employees in direct contact with customers should be empowered to go the extra mile to satisfy customers' needs. They also need to be provided with the resources to accomplish the company's customer experience enhancement goals. Gaining customer loyalty takes work. It can only result from a continuous and sustained effort to provide customers with an excellent value proposition and an enjoyable customer experience. Obtaining customer feedback is very important, and appropriate changes must be implemented based on the input. This feedback would help close the feedback loop.

The ultimate objective of enhanced customer experience is the creation of value. Therefore, the different facets of the improved customer experience must be explicitly linked to value creation by specifying the desired outcomes. Besides, executives must focus on customer satisfaction matters with the most significant payback. This approach will ensure tangible value creation benefits and justify the investment of resources into the enhanced customer experience endeavor.

We need to recognize that an essential factor can harm the goal of providing an enhanced customer experience. It is incivility in the workplace. Hurtful workplace behavior can negatively affect performance, lower productivity, increase employee turnover, and adversely affect customer relationships. Whatever the underlying causes, incivility in the workplace can increase employees' stress levels. Incivility in the workplace stifles helpfulness and collaboration. Civility in the workplace, on the other hand, enhances contributions and team performance. It enables team environments to become trusting, respectful, and comfortable places to take risks.

Companies today are buffeted by the winds of change and the onslaught of global competition. Injecting more civility in the organization can help companies navigate today's business world's uncertainty, turbulence, and volatility. Employees treated with dignity and respect are much more motivated to embrace and propel change. Civility in an organization will also result in enhanced customer experience.

Therefore, civility should be woven into the fabric of an organization.

Strategies to Enhance Customer Experience

Perception and desire usually drive buying decisions. Companies that create a positive impression among consumers about their products and who can quickly cater to customers' needs succeed in garnering business. Customers' desires must be satisfied promptly and seamlessly. Therefore, operational efficiency is critically important in this context. Companies must focus on fast delivery, minimal friction, flexibility, and precise execution. Exceptional customer service must back these attributes. This strategy is the winning formula that Amazon has perfected and is critical to its success.

To successfully execute this strategy, companies need to pay close attention to what the customer wants and make the buying process quick and easy. Customers these days need more time and patience. A complicated buying process will turn off customers and result in lost sales. Apart from Amazon, Uber, and Lyft are two companies that have succeeded due to their ability to respond to customers' needs quickly.

Another strategy that some companies use to enhance customer experience is to make the buying process painless and secure. This approach provides a personalized recommendation of products and services that companies can quickly deliver to the customer. Many customers like this approach because they appreciate the advice and the fact that they make the final buying decision. Amazon uses this strategy very effectively. This strategy not only makes customers happy but also creates efficiency benefits for companies by directing customers toward products and services that companies can quickly provide at that time. Customers feel empowered by the fact that they get to make the final purchase decision.

The customer-experience-enhancing strategies outlined above require customers to know their needs. Some companies have taken the extra step of proactively nudging customers and reminding them of their needs. Then, they seamlessly, quickly, and efficiently help the customers to complete the buying process. This strategy works best with customers needing more time and nudging. The companies that use this strategy try to discern the customer's needs by leveraging the power of big data and analyzing information gleaned from previous customer interactions with the company. For this strategy to be successful, companies need to have a deep understanding of customer needs. However, this strategy hinges on the company's ability to receive information from its customers regularly. Technology, such as wearable devices, is facilitating the information flow. This strategy also builds trust and encourages customers to go ahead and make the buying decision.

The last customer-experience-enhancing strategy involves automatically fulfilling customers' needs, even before they have become aware of them. Information from customers' devices continually flows to the company, which can automatically take care of the customers' needs. This system can be successful only if the customer trusts the company and is willing to share information with the company continually. There is much buzz these days about "the Internet of Things." Internet-enabled, "smart" machines can continuously provide the manufacturer with information to help fulfill customers' needs. The Apple watch has an automatic fall detection capability built into it. It can detect when the wearer has had a fall and communicate the wearer's location to emergency responders to provide immediate medical assistance.

The automatic fulfillment of customer needs strategy is contingent upon the customer's willingness to share data with the manufacturer. Some people with privacy concerns may not be in favor of this strategy. Companies need to earn the trust of customers. They must reassure customers that they will safeguard their privacy and not misuse the information gathered. Trust, once broken, will be tough to regain.

Stand-alone experiences, no matter how good, will not suffice. Companies need to convert them into long-term valuable relationships. Only then will a company be able to gain a sustainable competitive advantage. Amazon has perfected this repeat strategy by matching an individual customer's needs with its portfolio of products and services. The data gleaned from the needs of individual customers can also help a company adjust its portfolio of products and services at the macro level.

Understanding customers' needs and providing a seamless, delightful buying experience will make the customer more inclined to return to the company for their needs in the future. And every time a customer interacts with a company, data is generated. A company can use this data to better customize its offerings in the future and create products and services desired by customers. The agility in quickly meeting the needs of the customer now and in the future will be the key to creating a long-term competitive advantage.

Companies may need to combine the above strategies to enhance customer experience, eventually leading to value creation. However, we must recognize that no "one size fits all" exists in this context. The strategies to enhance customer experience must be formulated considering the characteristics of the industry in which the company operates.

Perception Management

It is said that people react, usually not in accordance with reality, but according to their perception of reality. Therefore, for a company to succeed, it must create a favorable perception in the minds of potential customers about itself and its products. Perception management is a critical element in ensuring a company's success. Brand building and advertising play a crucial role in creating a favorable perception. Brand building will lead to awareness and enhance trust. Effective advertising involves associating feelings or emotions with a product. Once the customer associates a feeling or emotion with a product, they would be more inclined to purchase it. So, the advertising strategy should focus more on feelings or emotions than the product itself. For example, one of the tag lines for Coca-Cola advertisements is "Open Happiness." Therefore, happiness is the feeling/emotion associated with the product. Similarly, the feeling or emotion associated with Marlboro cigarettes is manliness or machoism.

What about products that are intermediaries? In other words, they are not the end product to the consumer. Automobile castings or computer chips would be good examples. In this case, the focus of the advertising should be to create a perception of trust in the brand. Intel was able to do this with its successful "Intel Inside" campaign.

Perceptions of product quality also trigger buying decisions. Brand building and targeted advertising help to create a positive perception of product quality. Businesses whose products and services are perceived to be of superior quality are generally more profitable than businesses whose products and services are perceived to be of inferior quality. Ladies' handbag brands such as Chanel, Prada, and Louis Vuitton are prime examples. These companies have invested heavily in brand building. This strategy has helped them to create the perception of superior quality. This perception allows these companies to charge an ultra-premium price for their products. Kellogg is able to charge a premium price for its products due to the perception that it has created in the customers' minds that its branded cereals are of superior quality compared to the store brands.

Higher profitability is achieved via relatively higher margins because businesses with superior products and services can avoid price competition. This strategy allows them to protect their margins from being squeezed by competitive downward pricing.

An analogy to Perception Management is Managing Expectations. A company's performance in the stock market is driven by changes in the stock market's expectations, not just the company's actual performance. The higher the stock market's expectations for a company's share price become the better a company must perform to keep up.

For example, Home Depot lost half the value of its shares from 1999 to 2009, despite growing revenues by 11 percent a year at an attractive Return on Invested Capital (ROIC). The decline in value is primarily due to Home Depot's unsustainably high value in 1999 of $132 billion. Home Depot would have to grow its revenues by 26 percent annually for fifteen years to justify this value. This growth rate is *almost impossible* in a highly competitive business environment.

On the other hand, the German company Continental AG's shareholders benefited from low expectations at the beginning of 2003 when Continental's P/E was about six. Over the next three years, the shareholders earned returns of 74 percent per year. About one-third of the above can be attributed to eliminating negative expectations and the return of Continental's P/E to a more normal level of eleven.

So, remember, a company's performance in the stock market is driven by changes in the stock market's expectations, not just the company's actual performance. Therefore, **managing expectations becomes a critical strategic imperative**.

Sustainability and Purpose-Driven Strategy

Giving back to society has been a mantra of many companies worldwide. But corporate social responsibility, if properly structured and administered, can become an important tool for creating value. For this to happen, it must be firmly rooted in the company's business model. A deep sense of purpose must drive it. This purpose will, in turn, drive shareholder value creation.

Sustainability must become part of a company's DNA. Financial sustainability, namely, delivering excellent financial results, is critical. Human sustainability is also important. This strategy requires a company to examine its products' impact on customers' health and well-being and restructure its product portfolio accordingly. Another critical area is environmental sustainability. This area involves curbing waste and exploring ways of reducing the carbon footprint. Lastly, talent sustainability is also important. Companies should carefully nurture their internal talent while exploring ways to attract new talent.

If properly structured and implemented, these sustainability initiatives can enhance revenues and create wealth for the shareholders.

Sustainability initiatives should not be just a public relations exercise. They must become a strategic imperative. Companies should adopt a purpose-driven strategy. A core team should be created in this regard that should report directly to the CEO. This team should be mandated to identify the emerging megatrends that will impact the company. After identifying the megatrends, this team must suggest modifications to the current business model to the CEO. Other recommendations include the investments the company should make and the talent it needs to recruit and develop.

The success of this strategy would depend on the support of the board of directors. Therefore, the CEO must give a detailed presentation to the board (based on the inputs from the core team). This strategy would help the CEO get the directors on board, with regard to the new path forward. Even if an activist investor tries to deflect the company from the new direction, strong support from the board will ensure that such efforts do not fructify.

Apart from the board, employee buy-in is also essential for the new, purpose-driven strategy to succeed. Therefore, effective communication of the strategy must be conveyed to all the employees in a cogent manner that will help them understand and assimilate the message. Every employee in the organization should know that sustainability is crucial for the company's future.

Mere communication of this strategy is insufficient. It must be followed by bold and purposeful action.

For the purpose-driven strategy to succeed, it must be consumer-focused and not just a fiat from the CEO.

Any new strategy or path forward will be criticized. Rather than shun such critics, senior management must engage with them and help them understand that the new strategy is essential to help the company cope with any existential threat that it may face. Despite this, if they are still critical, they must be let go to not impede the rollout of the new strategy.

A purpose-driven business strategy should be common across all the countries where the company has a presence. However, each country's subsidiary must be free to customize the approach to its specific needs. But this customization should be within the broad corporate framework and must be implemented with the approval of the top management.

To successfully execute a purpose-driven strategy, a CEO must build a support network and determine ways to respond to outside critics. It may be worthwhile to bring NGOs and critics on board as partners. This approach will assuage their feelings and make them more amenable to supporting the purpose-driven strategy.

A CEO's passion alone will not be sufficient for the purpose-driven strategy to succeed. It must be embedded in the DNA of the organization. Constant and consistent messaging will be very useful in this regard.

Every capital expenditure must meet the sustainability test. To implement this approach, a sustainability committee must be formed to vet every proposal carefully.

A good reward and recognition system must be implemented to sustain the momentum. Executives who meet or exceed their targets as specified in the corporate strategic plan must be rewarded.

Implementing a purpose-driven strategy of organizational transformation is not easy. Therefore, unwavering commitment to this avowed goal is essential. The benefits or payoffs of successfully executing this strategy can be very significant.

Business Transformation

(The authors thank Mr. Krish Krishnan, Founder, Sixth Sense Advisors, Hoffman Estates, Illinois, U.S.A., for sharing his valuable insights in this regard).

Business transformation has been recognized as the vital key to success. Companies that have not been agile and have not transformed themselves in line with global business trends have disappeared. Therefore, transformation is a strategic and critical imperative for any business. It is not an optional activity.

If we were to turn the pages of history, we would see tipping points across time, transforming every field that touches human life, making the world a better place. A closer examination of change in any field reveals that there has been a lot of research and development using a large volume and variety of data, based on which the solution is arrived at. Many business transformations— from electricity, radio and wireless, automobiles, and, more recently, the Internet and mobile devices—have impacted our lives in multiple ways and provided significant business benefits.

A successful business transformation needs a powerful marketer (Apple with Steve Jobs at its helm) and an organization (Google, Microsoft, or Amazon) that can invest the required resources to create the business transformation. This strategy works in most cases. In cases where the model does not flourish, the business transformation itself does not last long.

In the late twentieth century (circa 1992–2000), we witnessed the dramatic emergence of the Internet (titled the World Wide Web, the original Internet protocols have been used since 1973 by DARPA) and the infamous dot-com bubble. This wave's arrival was strong but it was unclear enough to provide a business model that could be replicated and monetized. However, the first wave of business transformation from the Internet saw the web browser's birth, the search engine, and an online marketplace concept. Another business transformation matured silently during this time—the mobile communications platform.

Since the advent of the twenty-first century, we have seen advancement in several areas of technology. Some of the significant developments include:

- Mobile communications infrastructure
- Mobile devices (including phones and tablets): the birth of Web 2.0 business models
- The advent of social media
- The improvement of search platforms
- Adoption of open-source platforms in data centers
- Geospatial data integration

These massive shifts in technology are influencing the behaviors of people and businesses. From an individual perspective, consumers discovered the benefit of the Internet via mobile devices and found a virtual world where they could form virtual communities based on common interests.

As these virtual communities developed, community-based problem-solving became a central focus area of many of these communities, and a level of trust was established within the community. The idea snowballed, and many such communities were formed. Once social media platforms like Facebook and other sharing sites started developing, the communities' growth went viral. Soon, there was a community to answer anything on any subject across the globe. The interest permeated to professional circles with sites such as LinkedIn and Plaxo. The growth of these communities led to the following impacts or influences on businesses:

Long tail: The long tail is a term coined by Chris Anderson, where he explains how businesses started experiencing a longer and sustained tail of revenue and growth when they were able to market to a more extensive list of customers or prospects with niche products and services at competitive price points and providing better revenue. Another excellent example of long-tail involves fund-raising efforts and social media in the presidential elections in the United States in 2008 and 2012 by President Obama's campaign.

Crowdsourcing: Through community formation, businesses have identified potential opportunities for involving the leaders and trendsetters in these communities to become their brand ambassadors and provide irreplaceable word-of-mouth marketing for their products and services. Several initiatives have been sponsored by businesses to support this, and some have even created innovative portals for consumers to contribute to ideation and product design.

Gamification strategies: Another strategy by businesses to foster business transformation and create trust in their communities is the gamification strategy, where leaders are often rewarded for their contributions. This strategy helps deepen interactions with the community, builds trust, and ultimately results in the creation of value by businesses.

Open business transformation: By aligning themselves with emerging trends, some companies have invited the general public to solve complex problems using mathematical models or other scientific/non-scientific techniques for prize money.

While these trends and their associated models are becoming apparent, two significant problems need to be understood:

- There are many data of different types available for consumption by businesses today. The data is produced or generated at a furious pace and is commonly called big data.
- Not all big data problems are solvable by strategies discussed so far. The critical question, therefore, is: How does big data impact business transformation?

To understand this issue, let us look at the history of business transformation. For many, many years, business transformations have happened. However, until electronics were discovered and the first generation of computers were deployed, business transformations were happening relatively slowly. Enhancements in computing power started accelerating the pace of business transformation across industry verticals at a startling rate. However, the volume of data required for innovation has been a continuous challenge as most data was not incorporated into the computing environment in a structured format.

This problem was expensive to solve until recently. There are now technologies to process large volumes of data on commodity platforms for a fraction of the cost compared to the past. Platforms designed and built for handling scalability problems for search engines and social media platforms now provide the computing and storage platform for creating the enterprise computing and processing platform for large, multiformat, multi-structured datasets. The extensibility of this platform in an enterprise data repository may be a game-changer for many enterprises. Now one can access all the data needed to make informed business decisions, which creates fertile ground for business transformation of new business models and identifying blue-ocean opportunities within the enterprise.

Data availability empowers the creation of business scenarios and replays the outcomes using the data and the underlying infrastructure. Multiple scenarios called experiments will provide outcomes, and by creating the near-perfect experiment, you can predict the closest result to what your business expects. This experiment will allow you to create the right segmentation strategy for your customer, the right market for your product, or the right cross-sell strategy for your call center. The most significant transformation that can be brought to bear is its overall approach to prospects or customers. Instead of asking about the "lifetime value of the customer" or "the profitability segment of the prospect," the question has shifted to, "What is the value of me (the business) to the customer or prospect?" This introspection has provided the business with opportunities to adapt to different types of customers, offer personalized levels of marketing and services, and directly increase the revenue from such an engagement.

There is much complexity in this process that is not trivial. However, if the business wants to increase its profitability and remain in business, it is forced to transform its thinking and behavior. This strategy can be implemented most effectively with the correct set of insights and metrics provided using big data or collaboration platforms and a robust analytical model set.

Business Expectations Questionnaire

Formulating the following questions and getting insights from the business teams before starting the transformation would be helpful.

Vision

- Discuss the data, analytics, and artificial intelligence project objectives and overall status.
- Discuss interview goals (e.g., focus on business requirements) and interview flow segmented by who, what, when, where, why, and how.
- Describe the next steps following the interview.

Sponsor

- Describe your organization and its relationship to the rest of the company.
- What are your primary responsibilities?
- In that order, what are critical success factors for your enterprise, yourself, and your team?

Business Objectives

- Objectives, Goals, and Success Factors recap and alignment. Each sponsor and executive decision-maker must be interviewed separately for this.
- From your perspective, what drives your business to success?
- What business objectives and outcomes are you trying to accomplish?
- What are your top priority business goals by quarter for this year?

Metrics and KPIs

- How do you know that your business is doing well?
- What are the metrics that identify if your business is successful?
- How often do you measure these critical success factors?

Departments and Outcomes

- What functions and departments within the organization are crucial to ensuring the achievement of these critical success factors?
- How do they collaborate to ensure success?
- What risks and pitfalls have been overcome or documented?

Issues and Pain Points

- What prevents you from meeting your business objectives and outcomes?
- What's the impact of these issues on the success of the organization? Financially and marketplace-wise?
- How do you identify potential problems/exceptions or know you're headed for trouble?
- What do you see as opportunities for additional profit that are not being addressed today?

Competition

- In your opinion, what can your competition do that you cannot?
- Where do you stand compared to your competition in information technology?
- Are you able to respond quickly to changes in the market conditions?
- Are you able to measure and ensure the productivity of your staff?

Analysis

- What role does data analysis play in your and other managers' decisions to run the business?

Key Data

- What essential information and insights are required to make your decisions to achieve your goals and overcome obstacles?
- How do you get this information today?
- Is there other information that is not available to you today that you believe would have a significant impact on helping meet your goals?

Data Quality

- Is there data you would like to execute and report on but is not currently available? for reports?
- Are data elements reported consistently throughout the organization?
- Are there known issues present in the warehouse's existing data set?
- Is reporting data available promptly?
- What is the financial impact of the data quality issues mentioned above?

Analytics

- What analytic capabilities need to be implemented?
- How frequently would you review these analytics?
- What is the financial impact of having real-time analytics?
- What opportunities exist to improve your business based on improved access to the information?
- How do you see your enterprise utilizing the analytics environment in one year? Five years?
- What outcomes and interactive insights would you like to do with the analytic models and insights?

Summary

- What must this project accomplish in order to be deemed successful? Criteria must be measurable.
- What insights do you need from streaming data?
- Describe the next steps and opportunities for user involvement.

As you can see, we are just scratching the surface when implementing and monetizing data and delivering transformations in business. This development is just the beginning, and the possibilities are infinite. Becoming data-centric empowers the business transformation process and provides a scalable platform to create multiple successful strategies from one statistical model or experiment. The most significant risk is not doing anything. In the hyper-competitive business environment that we see today, not doing anything is not an option.

Remember the bottom line: For business transformation to occur and flourish, people are the most significant success factors, both from an executive and business user perspective. Remember that the actions and outcomes need to be minor, incremental steps. If not planned appropriately, the initiative may fail, ultimately leading to value destruction.

An example of business transformation came into being with the COVID-19 pandemic. Pharmacies based on physical locations and which dispensed medical prescriptions found an opportunity to retain customers by delivering prescription medications by mail. This strategy enabled them to provide a valuable service to customers. While not all customers enjoyed the prescription benefits, the services were used to get over-the-counter drugs. The supply chain documented the purchaser and their requirements for the medicine.

Quantities dispensed were not significant, and repeat orders mandated a prescription. Another opportunity from this strategy is the availability of people who took over-the-counter drugs and the frequency of such an intake, which can be helpful in other healthcare areas.

A recent business transformation story was noteworthy at a large automotive manufacturing plant where the vending machine dispensing eyeglasses and gloves for safety to workers started maintaining how many times an employee requested a new pair, discovering that some took up to five pairs a day. Some did not take more than one pair, every quarter. The supply chain vendor added the automation and provided the statistics to shift managers, who gradually imposed the enablement by adding a question to the second request within a specific time, thus reducing a financial drain over some time.

Today, we live in a data-centric world in which data is instrumental in implementing many transformations. Some have become significantly business-impacting and deliver value that cannot be measured financially. Examples include innovations like the Apple iPhone and iPad, Uber, and Lyft transportation transformations, and Airbnb in real estate.

We must remember to deliver the most appropriate transformation for a given period and measure its impact. The business transformation initiatives should ultimately result in the enhancement of firm value. If this happens, the stock market will reward the firm by boosting its stock price. Raising the stock price will create more wealth for the company's shareholders.

Successful Corporate Transformation

Many companies claim they are pursuing business transformation, but only a few succeed in this endeavor. Satisfied employees are central to this mission. They will be motivated to work hard and achieve the management's goals. Companies that invest in initiatives that support and benefit employees, such as DEI programs, and offer them excellent benefits, are most likely to succeed.

Transformation refers to a paradigm shift in how a company conducts its business. Some key characteristics of a company transformation include operational and financial restructuring, increasing spending on R & D, following an acquisition-driven growth strategy, investing corporate resources in sustainability initiatives, modifying its product portfolio, making a concerted effort to expand into overseas markets, and pursuing environmentally-friendly initiatives. A transformation's success must be measured from a financial and reputational perspective.

One of the characteristics of companies that have successfully transformed themselves is a high level of employee satisfaction. The employees at these companies usually receive higher compensation than their peers at other companies. In addition, they are offered stock options which act as a powerful motivator. These companies are also deeply committed to Diversity, Equality, and Inclusion (DEI). Women are also a significant part of the workforce in these organizations.

Examples of companies that successfully transformed themselves include IBM and Microsoft. Under visionary CEOs, both companies were able to radically alter their business model and significantly enhance their market value. IBM transformed itself from a hardware company to a software and services company while Microsoft transformed itself from a software company to primarily a cloud-services company. Microsoft has also built up a significant presence in the gaming devices and personal tablet markets. Both companies successfully changed their sclerotic corporate culture to a dynamic, inclusive, culturally-sensitive, adaptive, and people-oriented one. The employees were placed at the center of this transformation process. Both companies refreshed their mission to reflect the new corporate culture. The successful business transformation enhanced employee retention rate, significant stock price appreciation, and value creation.

Some companies have devoted significant resources to improving the financial well-being of their employees. Others have invested resources toward DEI initiatives. As part of their commitment to DEI, these companies have increased diversity in their boards and provided opportunities for women and people of color to rise to the top echelons of management. Both IBM and Microsoft are headed by CEOs of Asian Indian descent, namely, Mr. Arvind Krishna and Mr. Satya Nadella. Under their sagacious and visionary leadership, both companies have been significantly transformed and have performed exceptionally well. Significant wealth creation for the shareholders has happened at both organizations.

In summary, companies with an employee-centric approach to business transformation have succeeded very well and created value for their shareholders.

Cloud Computing

(The authors thank Mr. Krish Krishnan, Founder, Sixth Sense Advisors, Hoffman Estates, Illinois, U.S.A., for contributing this article).

Cloud Computing has become increasingly important with growing interest among various stakeholders. Cloud computing has come a long way from the 1980s to today regarding scalability, sharing, tenancy, security, and availability. We are all interested in learning all the potential benefits and possible pitfalls in the field of Cloud Computing. We will migrate and adapt to cloud computing, bringing unprecedented benefits to organizations. However, we must manage the journey cautiously and have evolutionary models to benefit each iteration.

What has made the cloud a choice for a growing number of businesses? How did cloud computing gain popularity? It all started in 2015 with Google introducing Kubernetes. Kubernetes is an open-source container management solution that provides scalability solutions using Docker containers, scaled up and down on-demand with automatic orchestration. The technology is so easy to adapt that all vendors in the industry today have adopted the same platform as the orchestration mechanism.

With the technology segment of orchestration being taken care of, cloud computing cost models have been assigned as cost of storage and computing cost. The cost of computing depends on CPU, GPU, and TPU usage. The size of data equates to its volume and associated transformations. This model of costing has made the cloud easy to adopt for many startup and midsize firms. The migration to Amazon and Microsoft was more feasible, although the data segments still takes a lot of volumes, and thus computing is expensive. The issue of costs did not start today. When Google did not even come on the scene yet, cloud computing was expensive due to the cost of infrastructure and processors, not that is gone. We have hyperconvergence, microservices, and TPU/GPU, so the cost's infrastructure side is a non-question. The cost side is from data alone. The volume, the variety (formats), and the velocity of its production and consumption are the target to conquer.

Think of the new computing model. If we can dockerize the data and set it up, the volume is contained in the container's size, total cost. If we need to scale up, the orchestrator will size the container and set the new container for a similar volume. This incredible model has helped us segment data required for analytics and machine learning so well that we can now get the cloud segment going. What about text data, images, and voice, semi-structured data? Welcome to the new world! Files are the way to provide data, and Docker is the way to itemize the same. Google paved the way initially with GCP and Natural Language Processing. Amazon followed several microservices models. eBay built and showed us Singularity, which handled thirteen-plus petabytes of transactions and retail services while not losing a single transaction.

The efforts from Google, Facebook, Amazon, Microsoft, and eBay moved the e-commerce space fast and well enough with many innovations and technological advances, some succeeding and some unsuccessful. Cloud computing is much more than a limitless expanse of servers and software we pay to use over the Internet. The cloud has become a metaphor for modern computing, where everything is a service that can connect and combine with other services to meet an infinite number of application needs. But to evolve this software complexity as a service, many barriers in infrastructure and computing platforms had to be crossed. Today, rather than coding anything from scratch, you can tap APIs to add machine learning, database, security, analytics, or blockchain services. Grab some open-source code from GitHub cloud service and stitch it all together, and you have a viable business solution that does just what you want it to do in record time. In 2021, businesses facing an economic downturn and the labor and capital required to stand up servers and license software being prohibitive, an accelerated shift to the cloud was created. In the IDC 2020 survey published in August 2020, 59 percent of respondents said their organizations would be mostly or all in the cloud within eighteen months. About 32 percent of their organizations' budgets are already being spent on cloud computing. This trend is accelerating.

While cloud storage offers many advantages, including scalability at the push of a button (up or down), accessibility from any device at any location, and pay-per-usage pricing, no free lunches are served here, meaning there are potential drawbacks. Security and privacy issues inevitably arise when enterprises consider entrusting a public cloud services provider with information that could damage the company in the event of a data breach. The system, application, analytics, and computing performance are other issues, particularly regarding low latency requirements and expectations. Managing data when locked up in the data center is, by definition, easier than managing data scattered across multiple geographic availability zones of a single cloud storage provider or even scattered across various providers. Furthermore, vendor lock-in is undoubtedly a concern when talking about moving petabytes of data.

Edge use case and security is a critical issue, especially when we know how Target and Home Depot systems were breached or when we read that over three million new signatures are added to breach systems worldwide every day. IT does not matter whether one is on the cloud or not. The fear of losing data and vital information is very much a thing today. Take Merck's case, where the London office was breached, and worldwide all systems, including laptops, were breached from that single breach, creating a settlement in Bitcoin. Financial losses are inevitable. Once a company is breached, it will also have an identity crisis.

Cloud challenges listed here are from our experience with the platforms. Remember, we migrate to a data center or a series of data centers, resulting in a spread or distribution in a data center managed as a service but still having a physical presence that needs to be addressed.

The main challenges are:

Pricing: Cloud storage is cheap, but nailing down your costs exactly to do accurate budgeting and estimate budget forecasts is challenging. In the cloud, the storage falls into three buckets: hot storage or active data that needs to be frequently accessed; cold storage or data that needs to be accessed infrequently; and cold storage, inactive archived data kept for compliance or regulatory reasons.

The complexity comes when organizations decide between Amazon's six storage tiers (Standard, Intelligent, Standard Infrequent Access, One-Zone Infrequent Access, Glacier, and Glacier Deep Archive). Similarly, Microsoft Azure has four levels, and Google has five tiers with prices decreasing as one moves to the colder forms of storage. The issue persists both before migration and then after migration. There have been several issues with the organization in the storage migration, resulting in delays in the entire migration. A recommendation in this regard is to create a bucket listing and add data types and volumes to migrate. This strategy will provide a rough order of magnitude of the cost models, which can be used as a starting point. Once you have these builds, a second sheet in the same workbook will be the migration of data across from one tier into another, where the cost of the move plus the cost of computing, when accessed, can be estimated.

Then, there are additional costs that organizations might not have anticipated. For example, the cloud vendors charge for data access (get requests and put requests) and data movement (egress charges). Business requirements constantly change, so companies may need to access data that they once thought was stagnant, translating into additional fees that the company had not planned on. Once all such incidental costs have been documented, they must be entered into separate sheets in a worksheet. Finance estimates must be added to these costs.

Adding a pruning policy to data that needs specific tiers and availability will help manage costs. One can move to a lower tier but access a higher volume, which means the cost is a wash. Therefore, it is essential to choose as needed and handle the volume.

Privacy concerns: Cloud service providers have made a determined effort to assure clients of privacy concerns. But privacy remains among enterprise customers' top three worries, according to IDC surveys. GDPR, CCPA, and other regional compliance and opt-out issues remain for privacy, addressed on premises quickly. Moving the same data into the cloud mandates a new data architecture. We recommend drawing the data privacy first on paper, segmenting the subject areas, understanding the provider's encryption and segmentation capabilities with whom you are engaging, developing the architecture, and storing the data with the proper privacy established. If privacy opt-out data is not needed, delete the same or apply your appropriate policy to the data and manage the same.

Management complexity: As companies move information to the cloud or multiple clouds, they face the task of managing across a mixed cloud environment, which will be challenging. First, IT teams might not have the right skills to check to see that SLAs are being met or to track the reasons for escalating usage costs. There are vendor-developed tools for many of these activities providing the needed assistance. License these tools on the cloud for a year, and one will reap instant benefits to managing complex tasks and learn that cloud needs one to break down the most straightforward levels of a difficult task and then sum the computing up as required. This fact is a very hard-learned lesson; one should not attempt to learn it in one go. Take time, but one will conquer the same.

A new model that the incumbent storage hardware vendors (NetApp, Dell/EMC, IBM, and HPE) are offering is a layer of software overlays that integrate an enterprise's on-prem storage with its cloud volumes creating a single management platform across a multicloud environment. Enterprises are emerging into the Cloud. Our experience has shown more affiliation to a single provider, even if shortcomings are usual in medium-sized enterprises. Due to their complex nature, large enterprises have multicloud contracts for the typical services they provide the best. Application integration in the multicloud environment will not be seamless, and efforts are ongoing to make this more comfortable as the journey progresses.

Storage requirements are increasing as companies evolve, and most enterprises want to get off that costly storage hardware refresh cycle. However, it's essential to be aware of the complexities of moving storage to the cloud, ranging from data architecture changes, storage tiers, volumes, increased data sets in the form of streams, and more.

The cloud is still the way to go. We are crossing chasms and beginning to see the layers of succinct requirements in privacy, security, cybersecurity, analytics, artificial intelligence, computing, and storage. The technology and architecture layers for infrastructure are evolving fast and providing opportunities to innovate. The biggest issue in this area is our information, which has value and noise. We did not bother much when we were on premises and built several silos of solutions. Now to move to the cloud, our information landscape is becoming more prominent. There is value in that, but it needs discovery that can be automated and run with several artificial intelligence, machine learning, and deep learning algorithms. Specific purpose data can be compiled for insurance (health, auto, life), retail customer behavior, loyalty rewards, fraud detection, real-time data streams from machines including planes, ships, manufacturing plants, digital supply chain systems, logistics, and CRM systems. These real-time information exchanges are well streamed, and managing with Kafka, Airflow, or Beam message broker architectures will ensure proper data landing.

The trends that are happening now indicate that we will demand a multicloud integration strategy. There will be an API platform that connects all the cloud providers. Of course, noise on data synchronization, granularity, security, and integration is a given assumption to handle. We will innovate and provide answers, but the duration of time for this to emerge is probably around 2025–2026. Who will adapt to that multicloud first? It will be large enterprises that have different contracts with each vendor. They will bring a load of issues to resolve, including storage tiers, data exchange, metadata integration, and many more business requirements to integrate and explore the information. The future is fascinating, and the opportunities to innovate and the challenges to overcome are waiting.

In conclusion, note that you can have the wings to fly if you dare to dream. Break the problem into a manageable and straightforward set of issues and solve them, and in doing so, you will build reusable components that can be launched into the cloud as services.

Mergers and Acquisitions

Companies worldwide, across sectors, aspire to create value for their shareholders. Growth is an essential prerequisite for value creation. Due to global competition's frenetic pace, in most industries' organic growth is too slow. Therefore, an inorganic or acquisition-driven growth strategy has become the preferred option for value creation. Therefore, all companies who aspire to create value should continuously scan the business environment and identify potential acquisition targets that will either (a) give them competencies that they currently lack, (b) help them to expand into markets where they do not have a presence, and (c) expand their product portfolio. It would be unwise for a company's management to think they can compete effectively by following an organic growth path. The management would risk becoming sclerotic and being blindsided by their competition.

According to industrial organization literature, the corporate control mechanism market is a free-rider problem solver to gain control over the industry by acquiring other counterparts' resources and capabilities. These strategic choices benefit organizations in at least two ways: increasing market share and obtaining control over product pricing. Multinational enterprises are more likely to choose inorganic growth options (mergers, acquisitions, joint ventures) as a superior market entry strategy to gain comparative advantage and improve overall firm value. According to academic literature, economic incentives have primarily influenced the twentieth-century market for corporate control activities. These include globalization, industry deregulation, financial liberalization policies, regional agreements, elimination of bureaucrat hurdles, technological development, international trade and investment agreements, ease of foreign market entry and ownership restrictions, cross-country trade linkages, greater integration of global financial and product markets, the establishment of international accounting standards and shareholding systems, corporate governance, and capital markets development.

A large number of studies in the market for corporate control area have described "mergers and acquisitions" (M&A) as an aggressive strategic growth choice to gain ownership and control over the target entity. This investment choice provides immediate access to target resources and capabilities. In an M&A dialogue, the successful completion of the announced acquisition and post-acquisition performance poses several challenges and risks to both the bidding and target firms. The challenges range from transaction-level characteristics and firm-specific attributes to national-level determinants that influence the deal. For example, domestic deals usually take fewer days to obtain approval from the local government. In comparison, cross-border deals require more days involving at least two different institutional settings. Because foreign deals are beset by various challenges, including valuation and payment issues, they create a complex process between the acquirer and target countries.

Therefore, the alliance and acquisition choice depend on the firm's characteristics, the host country, and the choice between product and geographic diversification. For example, a firm seeking immediate control over its host country's target resources should have deep-cash flows and experience with the target country. Besides, it must have expertise in managing global products and operations and must be prepared to face country-level risks such as political, cultural, and regulatory changes. Sometimes, a firm may need to pay a high premium to the target firm to overcome rival bids. However, the acquisition choice is a realistic "speed" compared to the alliance model in the firm's internationalization process. To our knowledge, speed in the internationalization process indicates the "time required to gain control over the target firm's management and operations in the host country."

Value, Valuation, and High-profile acquisitions

Regarding economics literature, value is a mutually acceptable point between buyers and sellers in a given market and time. Scholars describe value as the bidder's price for acquiring equity and gaining control over target resources from the accounting perspective. Value always depends on expectations. It illustrates that the acquirer has reached a particular value based on estimating the target firm's earnings and business opportunities over the next few years. Similarly, target management has agreed to transfer the target firm's control at a special price, the maximum or the best, among all valuations. Hence, both estimations are more likely to be unequal due to information asymmetry and managerial hubris, which lead to high premium and value destruction around the announcement.

There are three value variants in M&A dialogue: value estimations in the initiation stage, bargaining value in the negotiation stage, and realization value in the integration stage. First, value estimations in the initiation phase indicate a particular value that is an expected value of the target firm and a pre-finalized forecasting value of the acquirer. Second, the negotiation stage's bargaining value is debatable, timing, fixed, and adjusted price decided by the acquirer and agreed upon by the target firm. Last, realization value in the integration stage—a realized value out of actual earnings during the post-merger period compared to the target firm's actual value. Though there is no rule-based approach, the integration phase's value should be higher than in the initiation or negotiation stages. However, the value changes from one period to another due to time, the number of buyers, business prospects, and other firm-specific attributes. Further, value changes significantly for various reasons, such as local deals (information asymmetry and valuation errors) and international deals (tax and regulatory environment and foreign exchange risk).

Concerning value measurement, there are two approaches in the financial economics literature: stock returns around the announcement and assessment of pre- and post-merger financial performance. First, stock returns around the announcement are significantly influenced by the acquirer's valuation of the target and the price paid. Second, the acquirer's financial performance is affected mainly by its management of post-merger issues, including culture, human resources, market integration, and institutional and industrial environments. Concerning the realization value, the findings are contradictory or mixed. Some scholars argue that mergers and acquisitions destroy value, in which the loss is significantly higher in conglomerate and unrelated diversification deals. The failure rate of announced cross-border deals ranges from 50 percent to 70 percent. According to Forbes (2012), "Merger and Acquisition activity has an overall success rate of about 50 percent."

Therefore, we postulate that value destruction is rooted in two taxonomies: overestimating target firm resources and capabilities and the definition and measurement of overall firm performance. In particular, high-valuation cross-border deals are characterized primarily by acquirers with ample deep pockets, international stock market listing, investment-banking financing options, and prior international experience. A dialectic view is that business analysts must define and measure the acquisition firm's overall performance beyond accounting ratios and ownership structure. On the other hand, realization value in the post-merger period depends on the acquirer's firm-specific attributes and external environmental factors like business opportunities, market strength, economic and taxation policies, and political concerns. Specifically, the percentage of failure in creating value from overseas acquisitions is higher than that of domestic deals due to economic, regulatory, legal, and cultural differences. For example, Robert Sher, the founding principal of CEO to CEO, an advisory firm, describes that "most deals look great on paper, but few organizations pay proper attention to the integration process including post-merger corporate strategy, culture fit, and sufficient management capacity" (Forbes, 2012).

Case examples: Value Creation vs. Value Destruction

At the outset, we must consider that there is no rule-based approach where high-valuation deals produce superior value to shareholders and low-valuation deals produce negative returns. Hence, high-valuation deals significantly impact industry concentration, competition effects, product pricing, and competition regulations. At the same time, value creation depends on firm- and country-level factors and the industry's nature and degree of internalization across different geographies, such as the oil and gas industry. We thus discuss some cases that show value destruction due to unrelated business streams.

First, Google sold its mobile segment business, "Motorola Mobility," to Lenovo for approximately US$2.91 billion in January 2014. This business segment did not fit well with Google's existing product portfolio and therefore the decision to divest it was made. The irony is that Google bought Motorola for US$12.5 billion in May 2012. In less than two years, significant vale destruction of about US$ 9.59 billion took place. In this context, some analysts argue that Google might recoup roughly US$4 billion of the value destruction, after adjusting the value of patents purchased from Motorola. In the post-divestment discussions with the media, Google's CEO at that time, Larry Page mentioned that the company decided to divest its mobile phone division because of the "super competitive" nature of the smartphone market (Forbes, 2014).

Second, we can similarly find value destruction in Microsoft's acquisition of Nokia's mobile phone division in 2013 for approximately US$7.6 billion (Microsoft, 2013). Due to increased competition in the smartphone market and low sales, Microsoft decided to sell Nokia branded feature phone division to FIH Mobile, a subsidiary owned by Foxconn and HMD, for US$350 million in May 2016 (Microsoft, 2016a). Then, it announced plans to acquire LinkedIn for US$26.2 billion on 13 June 2016, which is the largest deal after the acquisition of Skype Technologies for US$8.5 billion in May 2011 (Microsoft, 2016b). The two cases reveal different stories of value destruction rooted in unrelated diversification and high-premium transactions.

Third, the Japanese pharmaceutical firm Daiichi Sankyo entered India by acquiring 63.4 percent of the equity in Ranbaxy for US$4.6 billion in 2008 and sold it to Sun Pharma for US$3.2 billion in April 2014 (Daiichi-Sankyo, 2015). Daiichi might have realized the value creation from the Indian and global market operations without adjusting the U.S. market's risks.

Last, regarding acquisitions by firms from emerging economies, Tata Steel acquired European firm Corus for US$12 billion in 2006. Subsequently, Tata Steel decided to sell its UK business due to its deteriorating financial performance. Other potential reasons include high-energy costs, weak demand, cheap steel imports to European markets, and union and regulatory hurdles (see "*Tata Steel plans to sell UK business as Corus buyout comes to haunt it*" The Guardian, 2016; Times of India, 2016).

Economic and industry factors affecting M&A Value

Institutional factors such as global economic shocks (e.g., financial crisis), industry shocks (e.g., oil prices), technology shocks (e.g., software, mobile phones), industry stagnation, or maturity (e.g., telecommunications) have severe impact on a firm's investment choices such as acquisitions. There were eighteen high-valuation deals in 2007 worth US$374 billion due to the debt market collapse and many debt defaulters. There have been several high-valuation deals in the oil and gas industry that were triggered by the plunge in global crude oil prices. We also find many deals in the communications sector due to industry stagnation or maturity. To note, Vodafone sold its 45 percent equity stake in Verizon Wireless to the parent company—Verizon Wireless, for US$130 billion in 2014. Some national governments have supported financially distressed firms during the global economic crisis. For instance, the Netherlands government bought Fortis Bank Holdings for US$23 billion, and France government-supported British Energy Group by funding approximately US$17 billion.

Since high-valuation deals are motivated by firm-level characteristics and good cash holdings, top-level management's strategic choices, such as acquisitions, aim to create superior shareholder value. This excellent value may come directly or indirectly from the announcement returns, increase in market value, product, geographic diversification, overhead cost reduction through layoffs, increased geographic diversification, overhead cost reduction through layoffs, increased market share and brand value, and acquiring resources and capabilities. For example, the Mittal Steel–Arcelor deal (US$32 billion) has significantly impacted the merged firm's market value and global market share. Kraft Foods–Cadbury deal positively affected product and geographic diversification. This deal was motivated by a desire to improve sales and gain market share. Secondly, although high-valuation deals produce superior value to shareholders, they still produce some hostile effects. These include value destruction to shareholders, loss of market value, overhead integration costs, dilution effect in ownership, integration conflict, cross-cultural shocks, and other contextual issues. For example, unrelated diversification deals such as Google–Motorola and Microsoft–Nokia hurt bidding firms' operating performance. Indian Tata Steel announced in 2016 its decision to sell some parts of Corus's UK business due to weak demand, European labor regulations, and poor financial performance.

Therefore, managers should carefully evaluate risks associated with high-valuation deals, especially those with unrelated diversification motives. That said, there is no doubt that, if planned and executed correctly, mergers and acquisitions (especially the cross-border variety) can generate significant value.

M&A during a Recession

The notion that companies must not engage in M&A activities during an economic downturn/recession is a fallacy. Creating considerable value with a carefully calibrated M&A strategy during such challenging times is possible. Some companies may struggle to survive and be amenable to accepting a buyout offer even if the premium is lower than expected. Therefore, deal premiums are likely to come down during an economic downturn. Companies should seize the opportunity to acquire assets cheaply during this time. During the global financial crisis, some companies with cash reserves deployed their resources skillfully and acquired companies at a bargain. When the business cycle picked up, these companies performed better than their peers who did not engage in such activity. The COVID-19 pandemic devastated many sectors, including airlines, hotels, and cruise lines. But this global health crisis also opened up a window of M&A opportunity. Companies with cash resources were able to avail of this opportunity after careful due diligence. Therefore, the strategy of engaging in M&A deals during a recession, after careful due diligence of course, can result in significant value creation.

Corporate Restructuring

While there is no doubt that mergers and acquisitions can create value when carefully planned and properly executed, we must also recognize that restructuring a corporation can also create value.

Corporate restructuring activities refer to actions taken to expand or contract a firm's basic operations or fundamentally change its asset or financial structure.

We can separate corporate restructuring activities into two types. The first is **Operational Restructuring**, which refers to the outright or partial sale of companies or product lines or downsizing by closing unprofitable or non-strategic facilities. The second type is **Financial Restructuring**, which refers to the firm's actions to change its debt and equity structure.

The critical question is, when does a firm need to restructure? Here are some scenarios:

1. When a firm is overleveraged
2. When a firm is underleveraged
3. When a firm faces sluggish sales
4. When a firm faces seasonal sales problems
5. When a firm faces externalities

Overleveraged Firm

Since debt is usually cheap, sometimes firms go on a borrowing binge. Consequently, they become overleveraged. This situation can eventually hurt a company's bottom line. Overleveraging may be acceptable when a firm is undertaking expansion projects (buying new plant and equipment, investing in new technologies) that have a high probability of achieving expected returns, profits, and, thus, return on assets (ROA). When a firm over-borrows debt consistently and has profitability issues, the management has to consider financial restructuring. Some of the options that a firm can evaluate if it finds itself in this situation include (1) Selling off unprofitable assets to pay off the debt, (2) Renting out equipment to pay off debt, and (3) Refinancing existing debt with new debt at a lower interest rate and conducting equity for debt swap.

Underleveraged Firm

The problem of underleveraging arises when a firm has raised most of its capital through equity. This situation could result in a low debt-to-equity ratio. The firm must continually improve its performance with a higher equity base to keep its shareholders happy. Besides, if the firm pays dividends, it must regularly allocate a portion of its profits toward dividends payable to shareholders. Financial restructuring options for an underleveraged firm include (1) buying back shares with cash (if available) and (2) taking on debt to buy back shares to attain the preferred debt-to-equity mix and renting out equipment to buy back shares.

A Firm with Sluggish Sales

Sluggish sales can cause financial distress, affecting a company's cash flow. That said, the line of business of a firm influences slow sales. Whenever there is an economic slowdown, firms that sell big-ticket items (high-value products) are afflicted by sluggish sales malaise. One of the areas most affected by sluggish sales is the piling up of accounts receivable and non-collection of credit sales. The cash deficit puts pressure on the management and forces the firm's management to take alternative steps to raise funds. The financial restructuring measures for a firm with sluggish sales include (1) using hedging techniques to cope with currency and interest rate risk, (2) tapping lines of credit to meet working capital needs, and (3) selling off unprofitable assets to raise cash.

A Firm with Seasonal Sales

Seasonal sales are attributed to firms in several industries, such as construction and businesses highly dependent on holidays. The critical question is how to keep businesses viable when the season is out. Seasonal pattern in sales affects company profits and, therefore, causes a cash flow deficit during lean months. The cash flow deficit causes the working capital gap. This gap slows down company growth. Firms with seasonal sales can tap lines of credit to cover working capital requirements during months of relative inactivity. Another option would be diversification of the line of business. This strategy would involve producing products with non-seasonal demand to compensate for seasonal sales and raising additional cash to cover the working capital gap.

Firms Facing Externalities

Sometimes, firms face externalities such as changes in currency exchange rates, global interest rates, and fluctuations in imported raw materials prices. These factors will cause a firm's product prices to go up. Pushing price increases to consumers usually affects the company's sales. This strategy results in sluggish sales. However, there are several techniques that companies can employ to reduce external risk. These include different hedging techniques, such as buying raw materials in bulk to hedge price fluctuations of imported materials, currency hedging, interest rate hedging, and futures and forward contracts.

Strategies of corporate restructuring are (1) divestitures, (2) equity carve-outs, (3) spin-offs, (4) split-offs, (5) split-ups, and (6) demerger. These techniques' common motive is the management's desire to exit a particular industry and become more focused on core business.

The choice of the appropriate restructuring strategy for viable firms is heavily influenced by (1) The parent company's need for cash, (2) The degree of the operating unit's synergy with the parent company, and (3) The potential selling price of the operating entity.

The implications of the above are that (1) Parent firms needing cash are likelier to divest or engage in equity carve-out for operating units/divisions exhibiting high selling prices relative to their synergy value, (2) Parent firms not needing cash are more likely to spin off units/divisions showing low selling prices and synergy with the parent firm, and (3) Parent firms with moderate cash needs are expected to engage in equity carve-outs when the unit/division's selling price is low relative to synergy.

The choice of the appropriate restructuring strategy for failing firms is heavily influenced by (1) the going concern value of the debtor firm, (2) the sale value of the debtor firm, and (3) the liquidation value of the debtor firm.

The implications of the above are that (1) if sale value > going concern or liquidation value, sell the firm; (2) if going concern value > sale or liquidation value, try to reach an out-of-court settlement with creditors or seek bankruptcy protection under Chapter 11 of the Bankruptcy Code in the United States or similar laws in other countries; and (3) if liquidation value > sale or going concern value, initiate steps to liquidate the firm.

Divestitures: A Checklist

- Does the firm have one or more divisions that are unrelated to the firm's core business? To evaluate whether the division should be divested, ask the following questions:
- Are the investment opportunities of the divisions very different from those of the core business?
- Is the business being discounted by the stock market relative to stand-alone firms' value because it is a conglomerate?
- Are there other potential benefits of divesting?
- If the decision has been made to divest the division, the following questions must be answered to determine the *form of divestiture:*
- Is the division viable as an independent entity that can be spun off?
- Is the divisional management prepared to lead an independent firm?
- Is financing to be raised as well?
- Which of the potential methods is appropriate given the division's viability (or otherwise) and your financing needs?

Summary Regarding Corporate Restructuring

- A firm seeking to **refocus on its core business and regain its competitive edge will want to divest unrelated assets and divisions**.
- Divestiture can also result in the division's assets being used more productively, as part of another firm (sell-off) or as an independent firm (spin-off)
- Several divestiture options can be pursued, such as equity carve-outs and spin-offs.

- Converting a division into an independent firm can be value-creating
- **The potential for value creation must be evaluated before commencing the divestiture process.**

Mission Statement

A mission statement summarizes an organization's vision, products, target market, direction, and organizational goals. The mission statement must be communicated to all and should be understood in its proper perspective for overall growth and progress. The chief executive officer should draft and finalize the mission statement as a blueprint for the corporate action plan. Drawing up the mission statement by himself or herself will give the CEO the confidence and conviction that it is achievable. Each organization must draw its mission plan based on the strategic value-creating objectives that it is trying to achieve.

Setting up Goals/Objectives

The speed of change across the business landscape is rapid and unceasing. It is likely to get more intense in the years to come. Disruptions caused by technological, economic, political, and global factors necessitate a rethink by companies concerning where and how they should compete, what business model they need to adopt, and where they must build/enhance competencies.

In this context, the chief executive officer has a critical role. Suppose a CEO can clearly articulate a well-thought-out vision and strategy. In that case, the company they lead has a much better chance of coping with the frenetic pace of change and prospering despite the vicissitudes of global competition. Therefore, the organization's most important goal must be clearly articulated, and everyone in the organization should be sensitized about this primary goal. Besides, a comprehensive set of secondary targets must be formulated. This strategy will give a sense of focus and direction.

The first task for any organization is to develop broad goals that individuals must achieve through collective effort. This approach will give a focus and direction for the actions of the employees of a company. The plans should address the interests of all stakeholders. The employees should feel a sense of ownership of the goals articulated by the top management. The goals should then be translated into specific time-bound targets for employees at various levels of the organization. When objectives are attained, a carefully calibrated reward system will motivate employees and increase productivity. This strategy will ultimately lead to significant value creation.

Working with these objectives, implementing them, and effectively coordinating all activities to obtain the desired results are the most challenging tasks for any enterprise. At the same time, they are also essential for the success of any enterprise. Earnest efforts and clear directions are required to convert these aspirations/objectives into achievements. Hence, it would be prudent for the CEO to constitute a core group of trusted confidants and charge them to implement the CEO's corporate strategy and monitor its progress. The compelling amalgam or synergy of ideas/technology/human resources/training **and** cooperative effort can ensure an enterprise's growth and success, that would ultimately lead to significant value creation.

Management Committees

To strengthen the decision-making process in all managerial tasks and for effective communication and implementation of the corporate strategy and policies, committees may be formed with members from various divisions/disciplines who could contribute effectively to organizational success. Further, it would help the CEO to gain insights from the collective wisdom of the participants. Those decisions are taken only after due discussion and recommendations of the various committees and not by the CEO alone. This approach would give some protection against any aspersions being cast on the integrity of the CEO.

Committees help widen the scope of knowledge and orientation of managers in various functional areas of the company and promote team spirit and trust. Decisions taken, therefore, will be easier to implement. The composition of the committees must be carefully formulated so that its members have a broad-based set of skills that will help effective strategy formulation and decision making. Furthermore, to maximize effectiveness, committees must be given a clear mandate and a timeline for the accomplishment of the tasks. This will give each committee a razor-sharp focus on what it needs to accomplish and the deadline by which the objectives must be completed. In short, management committees when properly constituted and effectively administered can be a powerful value creation tool.

Performance Improvement

Many performance improvement initiatives start with a great deal of fanfare. But in many cases, this initial enthusiasm peters out, and the efforts do not achieve their intended goals. Therefore, it is critically important for the top management to be fully vested in the performance improvement initiatives and pursue them relentlessly. It is also essential for small initiatives to be pursued because they can be implemented quickly by frontline managers. Besides, it would help break up significant initiatives into smaller initiatives, thus improving their success chances. The visibility of progress will boost the confidence of the workforce. This strategy would also lighten the load for the initiative leader and involve more people in the organization. This approach would build momentum toward successful outcomes. The top management should set milestones and let the managers take the process forward at the operational level. Senior management's micro-management is likely to have a deleterious effect on the initiatives' success and the participants. For the actions to fructify, it is vital to focus on resources. The metrics used to evaluate the initiatives' progress should be simple and easy to understand because sophisticated financial metrics can confuse them. Some companies appoint a chief transformation officer who is tasked with helping initiative owners meet their goals. While there may be delays, the initiative owners can mitigate the impact by ensuring the initiatives move forward each week.

In summary, performance improvement in any organization does not happen overnight. It results from a well-thought-out strategy formulated by the CEO and implemented by the senior managers in the different functional areas of the business. This approach must be a dynamic process. In other words, there must be a process of continuous improvement. Gathering feedback and closing the feedback loop is also very important.

The steps for performance improvement are as follows:

- Develop a vision and mission statement.
- Set up reasonably achievable and workable goals.
- Break down the goals into small, workable projects for implementation and focus on enhancing customer experience.
- Scan the environment, both internally and externally.
- Develop strategies/tactics for implementing and monitoring the progress.
- Get candid feedback.
- Develop well-designed training programs and gather evidence of the effectiveness of such programs.

Action taken in the above areas will go a long way to enhance performance.

Building a Robust Organization Structure

The organizational structure must be examined and strengthened to meet future requirements. Job profiles for all positions should be updated. A rational system should be formulated for better communication and control and to meet the challenges due to the expansion of the company's activities or due to emerging technological changes. Detailed analytical studies must be made with the expertise available from within and outside, including educational institutions/ consultants, to design or redesign the organizational structure.

Designing and building a robust organizational structure is of paramount importance for any industry or organization. The following guidelines will be helpful in this exercise:

- Definition of each operation and the skills, qualifications, and experience required.
- Selection of personnel with good health, common sense, appropriate education, enthusiasm, and an innovative spirit.
- Formation of committees for various operational issues to enable broader inputs and collective wisdom
- Establishment of better communication among the various tiers of employees to convey and understand the company's objectives, goals, and strategies in the proper perspective.
- Work-study exercises to utilize labor better, break the monotony, make the job more exciting, and widen skills.
- Fair, uniform, transparent, and unbiased personal policies are essential to build trust and confidence in the workforce. Motivation, recognition, and giving due importance to

outstanding contributions are likely to achieve the desired results.

- Periodically, it would be advantageous if the CEO addresses groups of employees on corporate performance, opportunities, risks, and company opportunities.

For instance, as an example, broadly, the activities in a large automotive foundry can be put/allocated under the following streams. Generally, each division understood its primary role and the role of other divisions.

- Production: Quality, Planning, Product Development, Process Checklists/ Manuals
- Technical: Technology, Manufacturing, Quality Control, Facilities Product Development
- Supply Chain: Selection of Vendors, Cost Build-up, Quality Control Facilities, Quick Response for increase or decrease in supplies, Confidentiality
- R and D: Process Improvement, New Process Induction, Quality control, New Product Design, Development and Speeding up for regular production, New Materials, Alternative Suppliers, Logistics, and Introduction of digitization in all activities where possible.
- Marketing: New Markets/Products, Customer Relations and Feedback, Quality of Suppliers, Changes in Customers' Quality Checks and Parameters, Alternate Supplier Products, Enhancing Customer Experience
- Finance – Accounting, Costing, Budgeting, Capital Structure, Variance Analysis and Corrective Action, Interest Costs, Systems Procedures and Manuals, Exchange Rate Fluctuation and Other risks, Indirect and Direct Taxation, and Digitization

- Human Relations: Recruitment, Training and Development, Skill Development, On-the-Job Training, Refresher Courses, Lectures by Specialists, Safety, Supporting employees for higher studies and Doctoral Qualifications, and Participation in National and International Conferences. Making persons sent for conferences and seminars to address groups of employees who were not fortunate to attend the courses in person on their return from such courses to reach the concepts/ideas learned and exchanged at such conferences.
- Legal: Compliance of Law and Risk Management
- Logistics: Transportation, Freight, and Packaging
- Digitization: Areas where digitization can be implemented, Tools Available, Adaption, Training, Storage and Accessibility, and Information Security
- Public Relations: Representation to Government and Professional/Trade bodies to voice difficulties experienced by the company
- This approach includes external and in-house programs for workers and staff to build healthier relations and share areas of concern in a competitive environment, the security of employment, an in-house journal, developing a sense of belonging and team spirit, and encouraging employees' children in their academic studies and honoring them with awards for exemplary achievements.
- Business ethics
- This strategy encompasses the quality and reliability of the product or services. It includes adherence to laid down laws of the land and refraining from unhealthy business practices. All employees must understand the importance of business ethics and that the company will not tolerate deviations or compromises that would be severely dealt with.
- Internal audit must be used for financial control, systems and procedures assessment, technological obsolescence

and technological gaps, legal compliance to minimize litigation, the safety of employees and property and against fire, adequacy of insurance cover/risk, and the security of information and property.

This approach can be made to broadly give the portfolio of each division for better clarity of functions. It will enable everyone to understand each of the functional areas' responsibilities to cooperate and support them for the organization's overall functioning and achievement of its goals.

Adaptability

Companies today are buffeted by various challenges, with the emergence of new technologies such as AI, supply chain disruptions, and increasing energy costs. These challenges have exerted much pressure on operating margins. Maintaining market leadership under these circumstances has become very difficult, even for established players. In addition, high market share does not now correlate with being the profitability leader. These vicissitudes have made strategy formulation very challenging. There is a blurring of industry lines, making quantifying market share difficult. Given the hyper-competitive global business environment and the frenetic pace of change, traditional strategic planning has become less effective.

Furthermore, the traditional metrics for measuring sustainable competitive advantage may be less relevant today. The ability to adapt to changes as they evolve has become the sine quo non for business success today. Companies that are nimble and adaptable are thriving while companies that are sclerotic are fading away.

For an organization to become adaptable, there must be a fundamental change in the **mindset** of the top management. There must be a paradigm shift in their thinking. The company must be willing to scan the business environment constantly to spot signs of change, unravel them, and take quick action even if that means making significant changes in the current business model. The challenge today is that companies are inundated with information. Successful companies are the ones that separate critical information from the noise, quickly process them, and adapt to emerging trends. In addition, these companies are levering technology to up signals about changing trends and acting on them quickly before their competition does. The real-time interventions give these companies an unassailable competitive advantage.

To cope with the complexities of today's business world, adaptive companies are using technology to test out innovative ideas in virtual environments in a faster, less risky, and less costly manner. This approach gives these companies a distinct advantage over their rivals using traditional experimentation and testing approaches. Adaptive companies not only focus on efforts to improve their product offerings but also expand their experimentation because they know that existing products, business models, and strategies can quickly become obsolete. However, adaptive companies also realize that experimentation can lead to failure. But rather than condemn managers whose experiments have failed, they focus on the learnings from the failures. These farsighted companies engage in a process of continuous improvement. This key trait sets them apart from their competitors.

Successful companies build an adaptive ecosystem that is grounded on trust among participants. This strategy facilitates smooth interactions between participants in the ecosystem. The success of these companies can largely be attributed to their ability to bring together the assets and capabilities of many entities. Companies within the ecosystem do not see themselves as competitors. Instead, they see themselves as cocreators of innovative products and services. They see themselves as partners working for mutual benefit.

Adaptive organizations create a conducive environment, facilitating knowledge flow and dissemination, genuine autonomy, risk-taking, and flexibility. This approach helps them succeed despite the changes and consequent challenges occurring in the business environment.

An adaptive organization cannot be built with a rigid, hierarchical structure. A flexible organizational structure with decentralized decision-making is essential. Truly adaptive organizations do not have silos because it impedes information flow and knowledge sharing. Adaptive organizations allow their units to communicate freely with each other. They encourage knowledge sharing, cross-functional collaboration, and co-creation. They have a conducive environment that fosters innovation.

With decentralized decision-making, adaptive organizations allow employees at the front lines to quickly discern the changes in the business environment and empower them to respond rapidly to these changes. This strategy gives these organizations an unassailable competitive advantage.

It is a fact that it is difficult for large, established companies to undergo a metamorphosis into an adaptive organization. However, even in such organizations, changes can be introduced to make the company more responsive to the changing needs of the consumer and rapid developments in the business environment. Even small, incremental changes can yield significant benefits in this regard. These changes include casting aside the traditional, rigid, strategic planning and forecasting process and incorporating risks and uncertainties into the model because such factors can adversely impinge on the company's performance in the future. Many companies claim that they are pursuing a range of strategic initiatives. However, to enhance the chances of success of these initiatives, it is essential to examine every significant source of uncertainty associated with each initiative. To achieve the desired result, a disciplined, measurable, time-bound path should be pursued concerning each initiative.

Adaptability is becoming the **sine qua non** for business success today.

Adaptive Leadership

Building an adaptive organization requires adaptive leadership. The top management in the organization must constantly review its actions and quickly make course corrections as needed. The learnings from the outcomes of decisions must be rapidly assimilated, and the insights gained must be used to improve decision-making in the future. A formal process of collecting, interpreting, and acting on the learnings from outcomes of decisions must be implemented. The organizational learning process must be open and transparent to achieve optimum benefit. Stress testing of banks is often done in many countries to determine their financial soundness.

Similarly, an adaptive organization needs to conduct simulations of future scenarios before determining the course of action. For instance, the COVID-19 pandemic blindsided many companies because they had not anticipated the possibility of such an event and had, therefore, not developed a contingency plan. But the successful adaptive organizations, led by visionary leadership, used the learnings from the pandemic as a catalyst for improving the decision-making process and making it nimble and dynamic. Knowledge sharing across organizational units was enhanced to effectively respond to a crisis such as the COVID-19 pandemic.

Usually, in many organizations, decisions are taken based on the information available at that time, which is often incomplete. However, as more information becomes available, those decisions may need to be modified. The leadership in adaptive organizations realizes this need and makes real-time course corrections as needed. Adaptive leaders recognize that failures are likely to happen. Instead of castigating errant employees, they focus on the learnings from these failures. This approach leads to improved decision-making in the future and boosts the employees' morale. Visionary leaders in adaptive organizations act openly and transparently. They encourage open dialog across a range of stakeholders. They dismantle silos that may exist in the organization. So, when the organization faces an existential crisis such as the COVID-19 pandemic, all stakeholders come together in a spirit of mutual trust and candor and collectively formulate an effective response to the crisis.

In summary, adaptive leadership will make an organization resilient and capable of dealing with any crisis that may suddenly emerge. This will distinguish such companies from their competitors. Furthermore, such companies will be value creators while those that lack adaptive leadership may become value destroyers.

Organizational Agility

Organizational agility is essential to survive and prosper in an increasingly complex and competitive global business environment. An agile CEO can help bring about the desired transformation. Indeed, agile organizations are resilient, reliable, efficient, nimble, flexible, and adaptive. They have the unique ability to be both stable and dynamic. This fact may seem like a paradox.

Successful companies build a durable frame. Within this frame, they build dynamic capabilities that help them to be nimble and agile.

In agile organizations, routine work, measurement of performance, and determination of rewards are likely to happen in teams that transcend formal structures. Teams are formed, dissolved, and reformed, and resources are shifted in response to market demands. Besides, performance metrics and targets are set and reset regularly. Cross-functional leaders are expected to meet periodically to debate critical decisions. Also, decision-making authority is delegated in real-time to those at the frontline. Collaboration across functions and geographies is strongly encouraged and supported.

Agile firms have recognized the need to redeploy employees easily and rapidly with minimal disruption. Functional heads in such organizations provide coaching and strive to develop the capabilities of individuals in their unit. This strategy enables these persons to move on quickly to the next opportunity.

There is always a silver lining to any crisis. The COVID-19 pandemic was a crisis of unprecedented proportions. Many companies struggled to survive under very challenging business conditions. But some companies turned this crisis into an opportunity.

For example, Dyson designed a new ventilator in ten days. Alibaba and retailer Zhongbai teamed up to build a personnel-free store for essential items and disinfectant supplies. Chick-fil-A developed over a dozen changes to its drive-through process to maximize safety and efficiency in the face of skyrocketing demand for take-out food. These companies and many others have been more agile. But companies need to maintain their agility even after this crisis completely ends. They should formulate agile teams and charge them with the mandate to generate innovations. They should engage people in changing the system through testing, learning, and adaptation. Copying another company is not prudent because it prevents people from developing the skills they need to adapt, customize, and harmonize all the agility elements. Tracking the response times between identifying a challenge or opportunity and creating an innovative solution is crucial. This period must be shortened as much as possible. However, this period is driven by the time spent designing a creative solution, obtaining the necessary approvals, and overcoming bureaucratic hurdles before the solution can be implemented. Streamlining the approval process can significantly reduce the waiting period. Besides, breaking a big project into smaller projects with rapid feedback loops will reduce the time from conception to implementation. Smaller projects will help teams quickly start the work and make course corrections as needed based on the changes happening on the ground. Such an approach will also increase flow efficiency.

The global business environment is highly competitive and dynamic. Therefore, to succeed in such a challenging environment, companies must operate the business efficiently and be willing to quickly and effectively change the business model. A business that does not prioritize innovation will fade out due to its inability to adapt. Simultaneously, a lack of focus on operational efficiency will result in low quality, high costs, and other risks. A company that anticipates a crisis before it happens and has an ingrained innovation system will succeed no matter what changes occur in the business environment. A flexible organizational structure will help companies survive, innovate, and create value even during turbulent times.

Building an Agile Organization

To build an agile organization/company, the CEO and the other senior executives need to do the following:

1. Understand the process of value creation

Determining current and future sources of value will help the CEO make the best possible use of the internal talent available and tap external talent as needed.

2. Determine the critical roles

The CEO and the core group members must determine those roles that significantly impact value creation and devote time and attention to those roles.

3. Fill each position with the right person

It is vital to identify the right talent to fill critical positions and nurture those individuals to bring out their best. The CEO and the head of HR must identify the specific skills/competencies required for each vital role. They must then conduct an unbiased evaluation of the internal talent available to determine if the essential positions can be filled with internal talent or whether new talent must be brought in from outside.

4. Evaluate performance and nurture talent

For each critical role, there must be a continuous performance evaluation process. Besides, internal talent must be nurtured to fill vacancies quickly. A periodic audit of critical roles must be conducted to remain agile and capable of coping with the vicissitudes of an increasingly complex global business environment.

Due to technological advancement and fierce global competition, customers' requirements regarding quality, timely delivery, and competitive pricing have become much more exacting. Under these circumstances, companies must focus on operational efficiency, cost reduction, capital structure, and technology upgrading. Besides, implementation of best practices, laying down systems and procedures, process checklists, work instructions, avoidance or management of waste, wastage of resources, streamlining of manufacturing processes, improving the safety of employees, being environmentally responsible, and complying with the laws of the land, are also very essential. All actions should be undertaken to create customer value while following ethical business practices.

To achieve these high standards, all organizational departments must work in unison, focusing on customer experience and organizational performance excellence. Therefore, in designing an effective organizational structure, various streams of work, duties, and responsibilities of each functional area become imperative and should be carefully addressed with systems to achieve the CEO/top management's goals and objectives.

The panacea for organizations mired in a bureaucratic morass and decision-making paralysis is to become more flat, nimble, and agile, with authority and accountability going together. Agile organizations can react much faster to the gyrations in the competitive global marketplace and take appropriate action. Sclerotic decision-making can be the kiss of death for any organization.

Given the frenetic pace and hyper-competitive nature of global business today, adapting to changes fast becomes critical. This approach is possible only if the organizational structure is agile and flexible. Managers must be trained to make quick decisions, even with incomplete information. Speed in decision-making has become a strategic imperative. Organizational agility has become of paramount importance. With fluid teams and less rigid hierarchies, an agile organization can reduce costs and increase responsiveness to today's markets. An agile organization can also quickly shift to an emergent strategy while unleashing its talent to reshape the business in real time. In a global business landscape evolving rapidly and profoundly, an organization needs to tap into a network of individuals, recognize the resilience a diverse workforce can provide, and deploy technology aggressively to create a competitive advantage to enhance value creation.

The CEO's primary objective should be a relentless and purposeful pursuit of value creation. They should encourage real-time decision-making. They should also move away from a hierarchical chain of command and create a flatter organization with decentralized decision-making authority. It will be easier for an organization to achieve and sustain high performance in a world of uncertainty where speed and disruption have become the order of the day if decision-making can be diffused. This strategy requires individuals at different levels of the organization to be empowered with some decision-making authority. Undoubtedly, prioritization and resource allocation decisions must be made centrally. However, many actions and decisions are best taken closer to the situation. A flatter organizational structure would facilitate this process.

An environment that encourages creative thinking and fosters innovative solutions to business challenges should be created. Leaders in agile organizations lead more by influence and less by control. They strive to empower the entire organization. The goal is to create conditions in which an ecosystem can be mostly self-managing. Individuals can learn continuously, and most problems can be avoided before manifesting themselves. Leadership skills at all levels of the organization are critical and should be encouraged and carefully nurtured. The CEO must take the lead role in the formulation of corporate philosophy. Then, the individuals in the organization must be aligned around these shared principles.

Change Management

The COVID-19 pandemic brought about a paradigm shift in how companies operate and service their customers. Companies had to reconfigure their product and service portfolios, revamp their supply chains, and restructure their organization. The critical element of this transformation, namely change management, had to undergo drastic changes. Organizational agility has therefore become a strategic imperative to cope with the vicissitudes in the business environment.

It has become even more vital for the top management to clearly and cogently articulate a change vision for their company. A compelling vision of the company's future, anchored in its values and principles, will serve as a beacon in decision-making, and the action steps that will be taken moving forward, are essential. However, merely articulating a vision is not sufficient. The top management must follow through on any commitments made in the change vision. Building a consensus regarding the change vision may not always be possible due to the paucity of time. Hence, it is better to roll out the change vision as soon as possible, even if not all stakeholders have not yet had a chance to voice their thoughts. It is important to remember that the change vision must be a dynamic, not a static exercise.

There are many pressures on the time of a CEO. In addition, during some unforeseen crises, the top management team becomes preoccupied with managing the situation. To free up the time of the CEO and the top management team, the task of dealing with the crisis on hand can be entrusted to a dedicated team in the organization who can bring a laser-sharp focus to the challenges faced by the company. This team must be given the support and resources to fulfill its mandate successfully. Suppose the required skill sets to cope with the challenges are unavailable within the organization. In that case, external experts can be brought on board to assist. This approach can be effective and more efficient from a time perspective.

Communication platforms, such as internal social media channels, can be leveraged to articulate the change management agenda and report on the progress of the efforts in this regard. Transparency in communication will build trust and spur cooperation and buy-in from employees.

While the CEO and the top management team can set the change management agenda, a core team should be entrusted with operationalizing the agenda. The head of this team can report to the board about the progress of the change management initiatives. The change management team has a critical role to play. They must be the champions for change management initiatives. As they implement the change management agenda, this team needs to know the pulse of the employees and other key stakeholders. The change management process is dynamic and not static. Therefore, this team must be willing to make changes as needed to operationalize the change management agenda. A continuous feedback mechanism should be set up so that course corrections can be made as required.

It may be prudent to switch from annual performance reviews to more frequent assessments to bring about quick behavioral change among the employees. This strategy will help the management arrange for employee coaching promptly. This strategy will also help managers convey to the employees what is expected of them then. The team should focus on those behaviors that are critical from the perspective of the change management agenda. A reward program can be set up that encourages employees to pursue the desired behaviors. It is worth noting in this context that non-monetary incentives can also be powerful motivators.

Change management can yield significant benefits for the company. However, it is a gradual process. It is unrealistic to expect change to happen overnight. That said, the management should explore ways to speed up the process as the business environment is uncertain and fast-changing. A company should be able to identify and adapt to the evolving changes faster than its competitors to succeed and prosper Organizational ability is therefore critical and a strategic imperative.

Organizational Health

CEOs should be as concerned about organizational health as their income statement. Organizational health is the company's ability to align around a shared vision, implement it effectively, and recharge through innovation and creative thinking.

Improvement in organizational health is likely to result in performance improvement. This improvement will, in turn, lead to better financial results and enhanced value creation. The top management should make the quest for improving organizational health a priority. Senior management needs to adopt a proactive approach concerning organizational health. A core corporate health team could be constituted by the CEO and given the mandate to integrate organizational health into ongoing performance reviews. Monthly and quarterly performance reviews should include organizational health goals.

The top management should endeavor and deploy influential leaders at all levels to improve organizational health. The corporate mantra must be of continuous improvement. In this regard, involving all individuals in the organization in a relentless quest for performance improvement and innovation is essential. The CEO and top management should shed an insular approach and prioritize acquiring top talent. Besides, the valuable insights gained through customer interactions must be used to drive innovation.

In many Asian countries, we see a prevalence of conglomerates. In such firms, there is generally a conservative, risk-averse culture. This situation probably stems from the fact that these companies evolved from family businesses where the "old school" patriarch usually made important decisions. Such firms must shed their current culture and move toward a more innovative and entrepreneurial culture. Such a shift will help improve organizational health and equip these companies to cope with global competition's vicissitudes. These companies must implement this strategy, improve knowledge sharing across all their business units, encourage innovation and entrepreneurship, and enhance employee motivation. As part of this strategy, the company should offer non-traditional career paths to those individuals who display innovation and entrepreneurship. With the complete backing of the CEO and the top management, such an approach is bound to improve organizational health. However, changing deep-rooted mindsets is not easy. Continuous effort is needed to change the mindset of the individuals in the organization. Employees may have latent needs, fears, and perceived threats to their identity. These emotions must be addressed as part of the mindset-changing exercise to achieve the desired outcome, namely improving organizational health.

The management should explore the possibility of building a network of influencers who can help change the mindset. Influencers may exist at all levels of the organization. A survey asking individuals in the organization to name people who possess influencers' traits would help identify them. The influencers could become powerful allies to the top management and help them by changing mindsets, providing feedback, and eventually helping them meet their organizational health goals. Corporate reviews must be built into performance reviews. These reviews will provide insights into how organizational health is evolving in response to the actions taken by top management. Good organizational health can make the company more agile and respond quickly to industry changes and technology disruptions. Rewards and recognition motivate employees to meet the top management's organizational health goals. A speedy feedback loop would help promptly recognize and reward high-performing teams and individuals. This process would inspire them to continue to act in a manner that is in the organization's best interests. Investing in improving organizational health is a worthwhile investment and would help contribute to value creation.

Organizational Rejuvenation

Organizations, over some time, become stale and therefore need periodic rejuvenation. Rejuvenation or transformation is a term that has several connotations. However, organizations committed to value creation define this as a focused, pan-organization effort to improve performance and enhance organizational health. When this rejuvenation process succeeds, it results in multiple benefits, such as increased top-line growth, higher productivity of capital invested in the business, cost reduction, improved organizational effectiveness, and higher customer satisfaction. The rejuvenation process brings about an internal alignment around a shared vision and enables companies to pursue a continuous improvement path. A strategic re-evaluation of the company's business strategy and capitalizing on emerging opportunities in the digital space would be integral elements of the organizational rejuvenation process. For this process to succeed, total commitment from the top management is essential. Adequate resources to bring about the transformation must be provided. Besides, a change in the mindset would be required to bring about organizational rejuvenation successfully. Corporate leaders must be willing to step out of their comfort zone and make the hard choices necessary for the revitalization to succeed. A half-hearted attempt at organizational rejuvenation may do more harm than good.

The CEO must believe that the organizational rejuvenation process will enhance the company's performance. The CEO must also create a "Rejuvenation Task Force" and empower its members to do whatever is necessary to ensure this process's successful outcome. A CRO (Chief Rejuvenation Officer) must head this task force. The CRO should have the authority and ability to bring about an enterprise-wide transformation. The CRO should be a dynamic person with excellent interpersonal skills and well respected by their peers.

The task force needs to devise a plan to change the organization's mindset and make everyone aware of the importance of the organizational rejuvenation process. The task force should also conduct a detailed analysis of the company's value-creation potential and create a timeline with specific revenue and cost targets that must be achieved.

Furthermore, for the organizational rejuvenation process to succeed, regular meetings between the senior management team headed by the CEO and the rejuvenation task force headed by the chief rejuvenation officer would be extremely helpful in moving the process forward. The rejuvenation process is not a one-time event. It should be a continuous process. It is worth the effort because, if appropriately structured and properly implemented, this process will result in sustained value creation.

Organizational Culture

While there is a consensus on the importance of organizational culture, there is no unanimity on the definition of corporate or organizational culture. It is the way things are done in an organization. It encapsulates behavior in an organization. Both monetary and non-monetary incentives can influence behavior. To build a strong organizational culture, the top management needs to reflect on what blend of incentives would be appropriate for the company. But this process needs to be dynamic and not static. It needs to evolve as market conditions change.

Visionary business leaders have built a strong culture in their organizations that gives the employees a shared sense of purpose and pride. When the top management and the employees have an alignment of purpose-built on a bedrock of incentives, productivity is enhanced. Increased productivity leads to value creation. Therefore, there is a direct correlation between organizational purpose and value creation. Corporate culture is also a differentiator between organizations and can thereby attract talented personnel who aspire to work in organizations with a strong and vibrant corporate culture. It will also reduce employee attrition. Building an excellent corporate culture takes time and resources. The top management must be willing to commit the necessary resources to achieve the desired results.

Organizational culture is shaped by the culture of the society in which the company operates. Multinational companies that operate in several countries face a challenge in this regard. It is challenging for a company to have a unified, monolithic culture in many countries. The cultural sensitivies of the countries where the company operates should be considered while formulating the corporate culture.

Organizational culture also plays a vital role in mergers and acquisitions. Differences in corporate culture have resulted in deals falling apart and causing massive value destruction. Two classic examples are the Daimler-Benz Chrysler and the Time Warner–AOL deals. Both of them failed primarily due to differences in corporate culture. Therefore, it would be prudent for the acquiring firm first to do a culture audit to understand the similarities and differences in the corporate culture of both the acquiring and the target firms. A plan to forge a common corporate culture should be formulated even before the deal is consummated. This plan must be quickly implemented post-acquisition before cultural differences cause fissures, potentially leading to the deal's failure.

There are numerous examples of companies that have pursued an inorganic path to value creation and have followed an acquisition-driven growth strategy. The problem with amassing a portfolio of companies in several countries is that each company will likely have a different corporate culture. These differences may impinge on the parent company's value creation objectives. Sagacious leadership is needed in such a case. Every employee in the company should feel that their cultural values have been respected when the top management is building the culture for the entire organization. A team could be assembled, consisting of representatives from all the subsidiary firms, and given the mandate to carefully examine each company's corporate culture and forge a common organizational culture acceptable to most employees in all the subsidiaries. This team should report directly to the CEO. This prudent approach to building the organizational culture will boost morale and enhance productivity, leading to significant value creation.

Building a Learning Organization

Companies today are buffeted by many challenges from all directions. Companies must confront fierce global competition, rapid technological advances, and sudden customer requirements changes. By becoming a learning organization, a company will be better equipped to face these challenges successfully.

A learning organization is one in which employees imbibe, create, and disseminate knowledge. Such organizations also have a conducive learning environment that facilitates open discussion and cooperation among employees. The bedrock on which the edifice of the learning organization can be built is supportive leadership. The top management must be fully committed to building a learning organization and willing to invest the necessary resources to make this a reality. It is incumbent upon the top management to formulate robust learning processes and practices.

A conducive learning environment is one in which employees can freely express their opinion without fear of recrimination and retribution. It is also an environment where differences are not frowned upon, and opposing ideas are welcomed without bias or prejudice. In such an environment, risk-taking is encouraged. It is said that true learning happens upon contemplation. Employees can pause and contemplate on their actions, as well as its ramifications in a conducive learning environment.

Transforming an organization into a learning organization is not easy. It does not happen as a result of a fiat by the CEO. It is the culmination of the top management's steps to transform.

Learning processes involve several steps: creation, gathering, evaluation, and information sharing. Experimentation is a vital part of the learning process. Knowledge sharing methodically is essential to build a learning organization. This strategy can be internal such as a post-audit, conducted after a project has been completed, which would be very helpful in capturing the learnings from the project. The knowledge gained from past experiences will be very valuable in the future. This knowledge would also be beneficial to others involved in similar projects. It can also be external, with regular interactions with customers to create awareness about the company's efforts to meet their needs efficiently and timely.

Enlightened leadership is the sine qua non for building a learning organization. The management should have an open mind and a willingness to listen to different points of view, even if they contradict its views. Leaders can build trust and cooperation by listening to employees without preconceived ideas and biases. Questioning the ideas put forth by the employees should be without prejudice and preconceived notions. These positive behaviors will foster greater learning. The cultural aspects of learning should also be given importance as there could be significant cultural differences across the countries where a company operates. Therefore, a targeted approach to cultural issues in learning should be judiciously formulated and carefully implemented.

The challenges of building a learning organization become even more acute when a company is large with subsidiaries in different lines of business. The reason is likely differences across subsidiaries concerning processes and behaviors. These nuances must be considered when planning to build a learning organization. A "one size fits all" approach will not work and would stymie efforts to build a learning organization. Creating a learning organization is multidimensional and should be treated as such.

The company's financial performance and the stock market reaction will determine whether the top management has successfully built a learning organization.

Unlocking Human Capital

Human relations—A vital key to high productivity

Improving human relations and making employees happy at work is the key to enhancing good human relations and increasing motivation and productivity. In many organizations, especially in the developing world, employees live far away from their homes. They leave their homes early to reach the workplace on time. They are usually under stress at work, being buffeted by many challenges, including the need to concentrate on their work, maintain the work speed, ensure the quality of work, adhere to laid down procedures and avoid risk of accidents. In these circumstances, employees expect something more than their pay packets to achieve a proper work-life balance and make the work-life happy and purposeful. Complimentary breakfast and tasty, nutritious, subsidized lunch will be an advantage and may reduce absenteeism. Management should give good thought to this need.

The CEO has a crucial role in making employees feel that their contribution to the organization is valuable and that their efforts will be recognized and rewarded by the top management. One of the core human desires is to be treated with dignity and respect. If the CEO and the senior management can create a conducive work environment, it will inspire the employees and give meaning and purpose to their work. It will help even an ordinary person to achieve extraordinary results. Recognition and respect are the elixirs that will motivate employees and significantly boost productivity. Enhanced employee productivity will ultimately create corporate value creation.

The management can convince employees that they are interested in their work productivity and holistic well-being by organizing welfare programs such as regular health check-ups, offering professional growth opportunities, and benefits for family members.

In people management, the key elements that will improve human relations are:

1. Treating people as human beings rather than as a bundle of skills.
2. Understanding people better and communicating effectively.
3. Making them feel valuable and vital to the organization.
4. Creating a sense of satisfaction among people

The desires of people must be understood to accomplish the above. Some of the genuine interests of any human being are (1) Courteous treatment, (2) Recognition of reasonable wants, (3) Security, and (4) Trust and Confidence. The greatest asset of a business is its human resource. Perfecting the art of managing this critical asset is vital for organizational effectiveness. It requires extraordinary competence, tact, dedication, sincerity, patience, and perseverance. Appropriate, instructive, and exciting programs for improving various skills, particularly the communication skills of managers, middle management, and supervisors, different types of methodology—seminars, workshops, interviews, case studies, team briefings, and group discussions—would benefit this purpose. Using modern technological aids is likely to result in the presentations having a better and more significant impact on the audience. When this process is meticulously planned and executed, it will positively affect the organization's objective for improving productivity and performance.

Most companies claim that their goal is to create value. In this context, however, the human side of the enterprise often needs to be fully recognized. The CEO and the head of HR are vital in formulating the right HR policies to help build an agile, value-creating organization. The CEO and senior executives must guide, influence, motivate, and inspire the workforce. This action has to be done with a sense of humility and without a dictatorial mindset.

The physical count of people, in total, is the population. The population with skills and abilities is its workforce. Human resources are an expertly directed workforce. Human resource in any organization is a very vital resource requiring utmost attention and nurturing.

Two companies may have the same technology, plant, and equipment. But their performance may differ depending on their employees' behavioral patterns. The bottom line differentiates between a good company from a bad one. In this context, the proper development of human resources is essential for organizational efficiency and growth. Consideration for people and their behavior is a prerequisite to any conscious attempt to manage people better. An organization consists of people whose attitudes have already been molded by parents at home, teachers at school, neighbors, or other employers. The middle-level managers' challenge will be to change attitudes, mindsets, behavior, approach to work, and quality in these people. They will have to identify the cause for their action, motivate them, and direct them toward the organizational goals. This task of directing human behavior purposefully to improve organizational efficiency offers tremendous opportunities and challenges to managers.

All companies claim that people are their most significant assets. However, concerning HR, many companies respond passively to the routine needs of the business. CEOs need to recognize that HR has a strategic role in the organization and uses talent to drive value. Companies should create Centers of Excellence (COE) in key strategic areas such as organizational development, talent acquisition, and talent management. Besides, line managers should be provided better support and mandate to work for the business's long-term health rather than get bogged down in routine administrative tasks.

The starting point for making HR a tool for strategic decision-making is appointing a **talent value creator**. This individual should be given the mandate by the CEO to help corporate executives connect talent decisions to desired value-creating outcomes. This leader should be entrusted with complete authority over hiring and firing, even though actual decision rights remain with managers. They should be held accountable using appropriate metrics that encapsulate year-to-year skill development, capability gaps, engagement, and attrition. They should systematically deliver analytically driven talent insights to business executives to succeed in their mission.

The CEO and senior management should identify those who can become strategic talent value leaders. They should then design a customized training program for these potential leaders. Besides, these individuals should be offered rotational career-development opportunities to help them become future leaders. A cohort-based, high-potential training program that balances rotations and provides dedicated time for skill-building will be beneficial.

Big data has become critically important for companies across industries. Assessment of data readiness is, therefore, critical. If appropriately used, personnel data can offer analytical insights that add significant value to HR. Without a doubt, HR is vital to this effort. Therefore, companies must establish a robust and rigorous strategic planning process that maps out the key initiatives that

HR will pursue each year to drive value. Besides, data analytics could be consistently embedded in day-to-day HR processes so that their predictive power can drive better decision-making, ultimately leading to value creation. Business leaders must be willing to make substantial data analytics investments to reap this powerful tool's benefits.

Management must identify critical factors for success or risks. A person behaves as per their perception of reality and is guided in action by the precepts they have acquired of objects and people. A worker who does not see a given work situation as dangerous will likely face an accident. The safety engineer may say that the hazard was obvious. Each individual tends to get a slightly different picture from where he stands and from his point of view and behaves accordingly. Different people may have differing images of a corporation. The image may be erroneous, but it guides a person's behavior. To them, it is the reality. Such images often provide the key to the understanding of an industrial dispute. Therefore, one of the key middle management tasks is to make people perceive a situation uniformly and how they see it. Differences in perception or contradictions should be settled by democratic methods— discussion, persuasion, and education. Wrong ideas should not be allowed to spread unchecked. Mistakes must be criticized in a constructive way. To criticize peoples' shortcomings is necessary to educate them. Therefore, managers' and supervisors' time spent trying to reach a standard view or a proper perspective of a situation is not wasted. This approach will significantly improve employee commitment to organizational efficiency, better understanding, and cooperation.

An enormous amount of practical experience and wisdom exists at **all** organizational levels. The key to organizational success lies in identifying and exploiting this latent resource. The success of

Japanese companies is entirely due to their approach to people management and workforce commitment. The major areas that result in a committed workforce are creating a sense of belonging to the organization, improving job satisfaction, creating a uniform and impartial approach, and developing trust and confidence in management leadership.

A sense of belonging can be created by keeping employees informed and involved. The need to be told is vital in human relations. Nothing can destroy trust more freely than not knowing what is happening and being cut off from information. The fewer employees are told about performances and policies, the higher the possibility of deliberate distortion or misunderstanding. The information must be appropriately worded for the listeners concerned. It can be disseminated to the labor force by team briefing or at each level, individually and regularly by their direct supervisors.

Besides, a sense of belonging to the organization and building personal pride and trust will make workers responsible for results. Pride in work can be significantly enhanced by making people feel trusted. Trust brings out peoples' best efforts to justify their confidence. Incentive payments create an adverse climate and destroy initiative. The time study and rate fixing bring about a "we and they" situation and induce confrontation. It is better to consider bonus schemes instead of incentives. Reduction in direct supervision can also build trust.

Further, involving employees in problem-solving and decision-making will improve trust and confidence. Giving workers responsibility for quality will also enhance their pride. The quality circle programs and suggestion schemes extensively and successfully used in developed countries like Japan may improve quality and productivity. People can get more satisfaction from tasks that limit their abilities or take them to new achievement levels or multi-disciplinary functions to break the monotony. Having a common dining area in the workplace, building company sports teams, encouraging employees' children to pursue higher education, and uniform dress at work briefings may further help team building.

Leadership Development

Only a few companies systematically scour for hidden talent that often lurks unnoticed within the organization. Sometimes, these potential leaders remain unknown due to biases stemming from gender, race, and other reasons. Others may need more time to project themselves, have backgrounds that differ from the conventional norm, or may have fallen by the wayside due to corporate politics. Whatever may be the reason, when potential leaders are overlooked, it is a wasted opportunity. This approach may be highly demotivating and can cause a feeling of alienation and frustration. Identifying candidates, who can be groomed for the higher echelons of management, takes work. A rigorous screening process should be used in this regard with the help of the latest tools. The selection of candidates may use psychological tests for politeness, modesty, and humility. One of the keys to sustained value creation is to institutionalize a continuous process of identifying potential leaders. Enlarging a company's leadership circle can motivate the potential leaders who are promoted and enthuse the people around them. In other words, there is likely a ripple effect. Motivated employees will also be more productive. A bane of many large organizations is the complexity of their organizational processes. This complexity can often submerge hidden talent. Some people are somewhat reticent. This character trait could result in employees remaining in the shadows despite having latent leadership potential. Their more aggressive peers can also push them aside. Despite remaining in the background, these potential leaders may perform excellently in their jobs, bond and collaborate effectively with their colleagues, and command respect. If the management does not put in place a systematic process of identifying such individuals, their talents and their potential is likely to be unutilized. This lapse can ultimately have a detrimental impact on the value-creation objectives of the organization.

It is unfortunate that in many large organizations, despite lofty goals of promoting diversity and inclusion, managers tend to recognize, reward, and elevate employees who look, speak, and behave just like them. This bias results in equally talented employees with leadership potential being ignored just because they look, chat, and act differently. Besides, in many organizations, senior managers use a top-down approach when searching for leadership talent. Some senior managers have the misplaced notion that only the organization's upper echelons know about leadership and identifying potential leaders. This egoistic self-imposed belief negatively impinges on their judgment and causes them to overlook talented, potential leaders. A subconscious bias on the part of the senior management can further exacerbate this problem. This flawed leadership development process can heavily cost the company in the long run and hurt its competitiveness.

Therefore, the top management needs to take a more enlightened approach to leadership development. A fair and bias-free system must be implemented to identify promising, talented individuals who usually don't make it to the shortlist. These individuals must be assigned to mentors who can groom them to take on leadership roles. The top management should also provide monetary and non-monetary incentives for employees who develop specific skills or competencies that the organization requires. They should also shed the "top-down" approach to leadership development and adopt a more "bottom-up" approach. This strategy will likely uncover organizational talent that may otherwise remain hidden. There is a direct correlation between how skillfully a company manages its human resources and its ability to create value.

Building a Leadership Team

One of the complex challenges confronting any organization is building effective leadership teams. Ideally, a team needs to be small but not too small. A small team would hamper decision-making due to a lack of bandwidth. On the other hand, team effectiveness tends to reduce if the group becomes too large, with ten or more people. In addition to team size, CEOs should also consider what complementary skills/attitudes/competencies each member brings to the team. It is also crucial to ensure that all members are team players who are motivated to work with each other to complete the task. They should not brag about their skills or achievements, resort to destructive criticism, or spread distorted perceptions of this effort.

For a team to function effectively, there should be open communication to work effectively, and there should be alignment in direction. In other words, all the team members should be clear about what the company is striving for and how the team can achieve the goals. There should also be excellent interactions between team members based on the edifice of trust. There should be open communication between team members and a willingness to embrace and overcome conflict. The CEO should encourage team members to feel empowered to take risks, innovate, be open to outside ideas, think "outside the box," and achieve something that matters to be organization.

One of the key reasons many teams are ineffective is that a lot of team time is frittered away in meetings that deal with mundane topics. Therefore, it is vital to ensure that team meetings address only those issues that require the team's collective, cross-boundary expertise. This strategy will foster a sense of purpose among team members and enable the team members to persuade others to work toward the company's objectives and goals.

Inclusive Leadership

Inclusive leadership has become a critical factor in helping companies cater to the needs of diverse customers and respond effectively to the challenges of global competition.

Many business leaders talk about the importance of diversity. But not all business leaders "walk the talk" regarding diversity. Inclusive leaders make diversity a top priority and an organizational imperative. They fully support DEI (Diversity, Equity, and Inclusion) initiatives and provide the resources to bring them to fruition. A common trait of inclusive leaders is humility. This character trait makes them seek feedback from others and give credit where it is due. They know their flaws and biases well and work hard to eliminate their negative quality. They solicit input from others in the organization that would help them improve themselves. They do not brag about their capabilities. They are willing to admit their mistakes. In addition, they strive to create a conducive environment that allows others to contribute and make a difference. They also give credit to others when appropriate. They strive to make the organization a meritocracy where everyone can be recognized and rewarded for superior performance and commitment to excellence. They are open to new ideas and suggestions. Team cohesion is vital for these leaders, and they strive to make this happen. Inclusive leaders also show empathy for the people working with them. They respect diverse cultures and believe in empowering team members. This strategy builds loyalty and trust. It also helps the leader to establish a connection with people in the organization.

Leaders who wish to become more inclusive can assemble a core group of trusted advisors who can act as a sounding board for the leader and give feedback on the leader's interpersonal behavior that may enhance or stymie inclusion.

Inclusive leaders recognize that they may have biases built up over the years. Therefore, they seek the help of people in the organization to identify and address biases and preconceived notions. Inclusive leaders see self-development as an ongoing process rather than a one-time exercise.

Inclusive leadership is not only good for the organization and for society, but it also makes perfect business sense. An organization with inclusive leaders in the top echelons of management is likely to be a more significant value creator than a company without such leaders.

Purposeful Leadership

Companies are beset by a myriad of challenges in today's fast-paced, complex, and uncertain business environment. They are buffeted by fierce global competition and a multitude of challenges. Steering a company successfully during these turbulent times requires exceptional leadership. There is also a paradigm shift in the nature of work. In today's highly competitive work requirements, survival requires creativity and constant skills upgrades. A leader's role has become much more nuanced. A purpose-driven leadership style has become a strategic imperative. A leader's purpose must be in sync with the corporate purpose. While this is a laudable goal, it is not an end. It is also essential for the people around a CEO to work for the organization's welfare as a whole rather than their interests.

When times are tough, a leader should inspire the people in the organization and give them the confidence that their company will successfully overcome its current challenges and emerge as a market leader in its field. In other words, a true leader will inspire employees to dare to dream of a better future. The mindset of the leader is crucial in this regard. Whether a leader can generate hope and motivate employees depends on the mindset. A leader should create a conducive environment in the organization that will elicit all the employees' support for the company's purpose. There are many stakeholders in an organization. A purposeful leader will make every effort to serve all stakeholders' needs, not just the shareholders. A purposeful leader will not fall into the trap of becoming an egoistic and pompous person. The purposeful leader will earn their trust and loyalty by treating everyone in the organization courteously and respectfully. In such a scenario, the employees will feel connected with the organization and will be motivated to work hard to fulfill the organizational goals. A hallmark of a purposeful leader is a sincere desire to serve others. Four essential traits of a purposeful leader are honesty, respect, fairness, and compassion.

Merely articulating what is right is not enough. Words must be backed by action. A leader must "walk the talk." Leaders must be driven by the belief and conviction that they should always do the right thing, no matter how challenging the situation. It is said that crisis does not build character. Crisis reveals character. Doing the right thing when no one is watching is not easy. But it is the hallmark of a person with good moral character.

In summary, purposeful leaders share many traits. Their leadership style will not only help a company grow and accomplish its financial and other corporate goals but will also positively impact society.

Coaching—A Strategic Imperative

Incessant and disruptive change is now the new normal, and what worked in the past can no longer be a model for what will succeed in the future. Therefore, the old hierarchical command and control method of management has become obsolete, resulting in the emergence of a new model. There has been a paradigm shift in the practice of management. In this new model, managers provide assistance and support, and not just executive fiats. In addition, employees learn to adjust and adapt to a rapidly changing environment where innovation has become the key to survival and growth. The role of a manager has changed from that of a "boss" to that of a "coach." In today's hypercompetitive global business environment, companies with foresight and vision train their leaders to become coaches. Coaching has become a sine qua non for business success.

The type of coaching that will help build a proper learning organization that will result in sustained value creation is planned and implemented by those within the organization. An effective coach is not judgmental. They believe in nurturing employees to bring out the best in them. They do not claim to have all the answers. Instead, they partner with employees to develop the best solutions. Coaching is not a one-way conveyance of information. It involves sharing knowledge as well as nurturing employees to discover it themselves.

For managers who are used to asserting their authority and managing by fiat, coaching may make them feel uncomfortable. So, they may stall adopting coaching as a management tool. However, even such managers tend to think of themselves as excellent coaches. This exaggerated belief in their abilities makes them reluctant to improve their coaching methodology and style. If someone questions them, they may go on the defensive. This type of behavior prevents companies from becoming proper learning organizations.

Mentoring is a form of directive coaching. A manager with extensive experience will share that knowledge with a junior executive who will dutifully and diligently try to assimilate as much of the information conveyed to them as possible. The problem with this approach is that it connotes that the coach knows best, and the recipient's role is to listen and implement the suggestions.

Sometimes, one-on-one coaching is not the solution. If all the team members are working well with each other and efficiently doing their job, it is better to leave them alone. Attempts at coaching some team members in this scenario may be disruptive and counterproductive.

Another approach to coaching is to draw out insight, wisdom, and creativity from the employees by gaining their trust, being a good listener, and building rapport with them. However, while this strategy may motivate employees who are being coached, it may not be easy to implement.

Another approach is to craft the coaching strategy to the moment's needs. In other words, this strategy is a blend of directive and non-directive styles customized to the situation. To be effective and create a lasting positive impact, a coach must show empathy toward the person being coached. In addition, the coach also needs to ascertain what they want to accomplish right at that time. The coach then needs to make the person being coached focus on specific facts. This strategy will make the conversation constructive.

This approach can be accomplished by asking the right questions and making the person being coached come up with the answers. Furthermore, the coach must encourage "out-of-the-box" thinking and make the employee take ownership of the plan. This strategy will motivate the employee to work toward the plan's successful implementation.

Coaching must be integrated into the company's culture to make a lasting impact and create value. The management should also clearly articulate why coaching is vital for the company from a value creation perspective and for the employees' success. It should strive to create a growth mindset in the organization in which everyone is open to continuous learning and risk-taking. Establishing a culture of learning in the organization is very important.

The top leadership team in the organization needs to exhibit the behaviors they expect the employees to have. In addition, the team should transition from precise questioning during the internal employee review process to a coaching-oriented approach. This strategy would remove the fear mindset from the employees and replace it with the trust mindset.

In many organizations, the regimented year-end appraisal process impedes organizational growth and prevents the creation of a learning organization. This approach has to end, and a collaborative coaching-oriented approach has to be adopted. The ultimate benefits of this strategy will be enhanced competitiveness and sustained value creation.

Lifelong Learning

Most CEOs claim their people are their most valuable asset and assert that their development is their top priority. However, many CEOs' actions often prioritize finances over human capital. This approach sometimes results in individuals being unable to get the learning opportunities they need to grow professionally.

The advent of Artificial Intelligence and Robotics has resulted in the automation of an increasing number of tasks formerly done by people. CEOs need to recognize that this shift toward increasing automation will create massive disruptions to employment and entail enormous implications for them. Therefore, CEOs need to emphasize **lifelong learning** because it has become a strategic imperative, central to maximizing their company's value and impact. CEOs need to realize that their organization's people will need to use complex cognitive skills more and more. Therefore, it is incumbent upon CEOs to ensure that the people in their organization have these skills. Providing information-rich tools is not sufficient. Individuals must be trained to use these tools properly and maximize their effectiveness. This strategy is possible only through continuous learning. CEOs must emphasize continuous learning at **every level** of the organization they head.

Given the frenetic pace of global competition and the structural changes brought about by digitization and advanced analytics, organizations must adapt continually. This approach implies that individuals need to learn while executing.

Since the future of learning is in the field and not the classroom, CEOs need to model learning behavior and invest heavily in developing learning processes and tools.

CEOs must ensure that learning permeates every aspect of the organization. They need to rethink regularly improving the skills of the employees beyond conventional training and education. They need to be open to experimenting with new learning methods. They must encourage individuals to communicate spontaneously and continuously and collaborate across boundaries, such as expertise or distance. This strategy will foster peer-to-peer learning.

CEOs should focus on and spend more time upgrading employees' skills in a conducive and collaborative learning environment. Lifelong learning must become the organization's mantra. This commitment to and focus on lifelong learning will most certainly contribute to the goal of value creation. In this context, providing employees access to the latest journals/books through an online platform or an onsite library will be very beneficial. Lifelong learning cannot be an arbitrary, ad hoc exercise. A comprehensive plan must be put in place in order to garner the benefits of lifelong learning. There must be sustained commitment to bringing the plans in this regard to fruition.

Hiring Talent

Hiring talent remains a top concern of CEOs. There has been a paradigm shift in the hiring process. Traditionally, the HR staff prepared a thorough job analysis in large corporations, including the ideal candidate's traits. Then a job analysis was performed to determine the appropriate pay. The job was then advertised in the print media. The applicants' pool was sorted using various skills/ personality/IQ, tests, reference checks, and detailed interviews. After this time-consuming vetting process, a job offer was extended to the selected candidate.

Today, the process has changed in many ways. A large number of people who are hired these days are those who are not even looking for a new job. Many companies have outsourced the hiring process to specialized placement companies. These companies hire subcontractors in India and the Philippines to scan social media such as LinkedIn and identify potential candidates. Companies that still conduct the hiring process use technological tools such as Big Data and AI to identify the right candidate for each position. A technology-based hiring and retention process has become a strategic imperative for many companies. They have realized the importance of the HR function from the value creation perspective. HR analytics can help a company identify individuals inclined to leave the organization. Timely intervention can help retain those individuals in the organization. Although there would be costs involved in this process, this option may be cheaper than hiring from outside. Besides, a focus on outside hiring may have the deleterious effect of causing current employees to spend their time and energy positioning themselves for jobs in other organizations.

This strategy may disrupt the organizational culture and impinge employee productivity.

In today's knowledge-based world, talented employees are an organization's greatest asset. Hiring talented people who will add the greatest value to the organization is a big challenge. But perhaps a bigger challenge is nurturing them, and creating a conducive work environment in which they can grow professionally and achieve their career inspirations while meeting the organization's goals and objectives.

The Future of HR

(The authors thank Dr. Raja Roy Choudhury, Dean and Director, Prestige Group of Institutions, Indore, Madhya Pradesh, India, for sharing his valuable insights in this regard).

The Role of Big Data

There is much talk about Big Data having taken over HR processes. But what is Big Data?

Big Data is manipulating vast amounts of data extracted from new technologies, structured and unstructured, to analyze and use its value in making better business decisions and strategies.

In the case of HR departments, Big Data is beneficial mainly in two functions:

1. Search and hiring of competent personnel per company policies.
2. Improvement of the working conditions of the workforce through sentiment analysis.

However, some experts consider that Big Data, as such, does not have a practical application in human resources. Companies do not have so much staff volume that they must handle large amounts of data. For this reason, many experts speak instead of small data in the sector to structure the information and extract the highest value based on the objectives of each HR department.

The Five Keys of Big Data

To contextualize the role of Big Data in HR, we should understand the underlying driving factors:

Volume
The main feature of Big Data is the fact that large amounts of data must be managed and processed quickly in an appropriate manner.

Speed
Companies need to process a massive amount of information quickly and in real-time to exploit the advantages of Big Data fully. For example, on YouTube, estimates show that five hundred hours of video are uploaded per minute, and almost eighty thousand videos are watched per second.

Variety
The analyzed metrics come from very different sources, such as cloud data stores or logging systems, in both a structured and an unstructured way. However, it is estimated that 90 percent of the information already comes in a structured way. That is why we see the emergence of platforms compatible with multiple types and sources of data.

Veracity
After obtaining the information, it is necessary to analyze if valuable references can be extracted since not all the data offered are of the same quality. However, given the amount of information that must be processed, the management must decide if this is an essential, mission-critical task.

Value
It refers to the potential profitability resulting from data management. Although applying Big Data tools means a high

economic cost; it should result in better performance, eventually leading to enhanced profitability.

Big Data is changing the nature of human resources departments. Due to this reason, HR professionals who know about Big Data applications in their daily work can acquire a fundamental competitive advantage for the company where they are employed.

The trends that are being observed when applying Big Data to human resources are the following:

- Analysts begin by studying primary data and results of established metrics.
- A comparative analysis of KPI, trends, and benchmarking is carried out.
- The next stage is included in the predictive phase, with a multidimensional analysis and subsequent modeling (forecast regarding the levels of rotation, real-time talent management to give quick answers, and chances of leaving talented workers).

Thus, Big Data can be applied in selecting personnel, providing valuable information when choosing profiles that fit the company's vision and mission. Similarly, it allows HR departments to know what factors can increase employees' productivity and satisfaction. For example, it can be used to determine why an area of the company has a significant turnover; or what benefits the employees most value and act based on this information.

In the long run, what are the advantages and disadvantages of Big Data in HR?

Advantages:

- Human Resources departments will increasingly speak more in business language. Measured and analyzed data will be provided, combined with the department staff's work as a rule and external experts such as psychologists.
- Decision-making will be based on data so that it will be less intuitive and more efficient.
- Based on the data, one can improve the talent search, train employees, motivate them, and strengthen talent retention.

Disadvantages:

- The cost of training or hiring companies/personnel to analyze data is high.
- The cultural change involves working with other procedures for human resources departments.
- Handling data involves a security and privacy risk, depending on the tools and forms used.

Human resources departments' great challenge is incorporating data analysis to improve processes.

Machine Learning and Deep Learning

The future of HR lies in deep learning, which is machine learning on steroids! This technique improves machines' ability to find and amplify even the smallest patterns. This technique is called a deep neural network. It has many layers of simple computational nodes that work together to search for data and deliver a final result in a prediction.

The inner workings of the human brain were the inspiration between neural networks. The nodes are like neurons, and the network is like the brain. Hinton (2015) published his pioneering work in this area.

Machine (and deep) learning comes in three forms: supervised, unsupervised, and reinforced:

In *supervised learning*, the data is labeled to indicate to the machine exactly what patterns to spot. Think of it as a tracking dog that will chase the targets once you know the wrapper you're looking for. That's what you do when you press play on a Netflix program: telling the algorithm to find similar programs.

In *unsupervised learning,* the data has no tags. The machine only searches for any pattern it can find. This approach lets a person check many different objects and classify them with similar wrappers. Unsupervised techniques are not as popular because they have less apparent applications, but curiously, they have gained strength in cybersecurity.

Finally, we have *reinforcement learning*, the last frontier of machine learning. A reinforcement algorithm learns by trial and error to achieve a clear objective. It tries many different things and is rewarded or penalized depending on whether its behaviors help prevent it from reaching its goal. An analogy to this is like when a child behaves well when praised and showered with affection. Reinforcement learning is based on Google's AlphaGo, the program that surpasses the best human players in the complex Go game.

Applied to human resources, although the growth potential is vast, the current use of machine learning is limited. It presents a dilemma that must be resolved in the future, related to machines' ability to discover human beings' talent beyond their complex and verifiable competencies, such as education level.

Software intelligence is transforming human resources. Currently, it mainly focuses on recruitment processes, which in most cases, are costly and inefficient; our goal is to find the best candidates among thousands of them. However, we can see multiple application examples.

A first example would be developing technology that would allow people to create gender-neutral job descriptions to attract the best possible male or female candidates. This approach would boost a group of job seekers and a more stable population of employees.

A second example is the training recommendations that employees could receive. These employees often have many training options but often cannot find what is most relevant to them. Therefore, these algorithms present the internal and external courses that best suit the employee's development objectives. These are based on many variables, including the skills the employee intends to develop and the paths taken by other employees with similar professional goals.

A third example is Sentiment Analysis, a form of NLP (Natural Language Processing) that analyzes the social conversations generated on the Internet to identify opinions and extract the emotions (positive, negative, or neutral) these implicitly carry. With the sentiment analysis, it is determined:

- Who is the subject of the opinion?
- What is being said?
- How is the opinion: positive, negative, or neutral?

This tool can be applied to words, expressions, phrases, paragraphs, and documents in social networks, blogs, forums, or review pages. The sentiment analysis will determine the hidden connotation behind the subjective information.

There are different systems of sentiment analysis:

- Analysis of feeling by polarity: Opinions are classified as very positive, positive, neutral, negative, or very negative. This type of analysis is straightforward, with reviews made with scoring mechanisms from 1 to 5, where number 1 is very negative and 5 is very positive.
- Analysis of feeling by type of emotion: The analysis detects emotions and specific feelings: happiness, sadness, anger, and frustration. Usually, there is a list of words and the feelings they are typically related to.
- Sentiment analysis by intention: This system interprets the comments according to their purpose: Is it a complaint? A question? A request?
- A fourth example is Employee Attrition, through which we can predict which employees will remain in the company and which will not be based on several parameters.

These four cases illustrate that machine learning elevates the human resources' role from tactical to strategic processes. Innovative software enables workforce management mechanics, such as creating job applications, recommending courses, or predicting which employees are more likely to leave the company, giving the possibility to react in time and apply corrective policies for those deficiencies.

From a business point of view, machine learning technology is an opportunity to drive greater efficiency and efficiency in decision-making. This technology will help everyone make better decisions and, equally important, give human resources a strategic and valuable voice at the executive level. This approach will ultimately lead to more significant value creation. Therefore, machine learning technology is a powerful tool to help companies create value and gain a competitive advantage.

The Role of AI in HR

Big data, machine learning, predictive analysis, and chatbots are new concepts that we must know and understand before jumping into "data" to explore the new types of artificial intelligence linked to the field of HR.

As we enter unknown territory, we must understand artificial intelligence concepts well.

Before discussing the terms, knowing what artificial intelligence is and its different types is a fundamental step.

Thus, a definition of artificial intelligence to approach this concept is "the discipline that unites sciences such as logic, computation or philosophy intending to create artificial entities capable of solving problems by themselves."

But is there a way to simplify the definition of AI? Yes, indeed. AI refers to machines that think like humans.

Once this is clear, we can then identify the most important types of artificial intelligence coined by Stuart Russell and Peter Norvig (2002):

1. Systems that think like humans—the systems that try to emulate human thinking, such as problem-solving or learning.
2. Systems that act like humans—the clearest example of this type of artificial intelligence is robotics. This case studies how computers usually perform tasks linked to humans.
3. Systems that reason—those who try to imitate the rational, logical thinking of the human being.
4. Systems that act rationally. It is the system that tries to achieve specific objectives based on beliefs. They have qualities such as reasoning, learning, or perception.

On the other hand, what are some of the concepts you should be aware of?

Literally, "big data" is defined as a set of data of such magnitude that traditional IT management tools cannot manage them. As a recruiter, you are one of the professionals handling large amounts of data: employee administrative information, salaries, and skills assessment.

Machine learning

People often talk about learning by example. This approach is the basis of machine learning. It represents the processes that allow intelligent machines to remember according to the rules pre-established by algorithms that feed on examples. As in any formation, one always begins by imparting the theory; examples are given, the rules are marked, and sometimes the exceptions are applied to the rule. Then, it is time for practice; the more experience we accumulate, the more we learn. Machine learning works precisely in the same way.

Deep learning

This area is a subfield of machine learning that gives artificial intelligence machines the autonomy to treat a large volume of data hierarchically. The system begins by analyzing the data in a simplified way and gradually refines the search until it reaches concrete results. During an interview, the first things that are detected are the primary social cues. You will know what we mean when we talk about these small gestures of communication that arouse your attention quickly: a stutter, a frown, a silence, or a well-chosen word.

These artificial intelligence elements will accumulate in your mind, and you will begin to establish associations that will lead you to form an opinion about the candidate. This approach will ultimately motivate your decision during the recruitment process. Deep learning can reproduce the same process.

Decision tree

The graphic representation of the rules leads to decision-making in the form of a tree. Each branch represents the different possible decisions, leading to other options and so on, until the conclusion. For each of the branches, there are associated probabilities. When you classify CVs in HR, you apply specific screening filters for each position.

Supervised or unsupervised learning

What distinguishes these two methods is the intervention or absence of the human hand in the machine-learning process. In the first type of artificial intelligence, a person writes down or classifies the data to create samples to guide the machine. Second, the computer will have to search independently among a large volume of data from diverse sources. An HR professional has many hiring processes behind their back.

From the pre-selection of curricula to the interview with the final candidate, all the information is examples of supervised learning. This information can be fed to an algorithm to find the logic behind your decisions and reproduce them.

On the contrary, the unsupervised one will not consider the HR actions and will organize the CVs in different categories (business profile, technical profile, junior, and senior) with the risk of making classification by irrelevant groups from a practical viewpoint.

Neural networks in artificial intelligence

They are algorithms that can schematically mimic the biological neural networks initially designed to model data processing. These operational rules are based on statistics and are learned as they occur. For example, they are applied to recognizing shapes and images, stock markets, or medical diagnoses. When you receive a candidate in an interview, he offers you much information (their degrees, experience, technical skills). Each of your neurons will apply mysterious mathematical formulas that will weigh each piece of information based on your conscious and unconscious expectations to allow you to decide whether the candidate continues in the process or not. Natural language processing (PLN) is a form of artificial intelligence that becomes the crossroads between linguistics and computer science. It is the field that combines information technologies (among which is artificial intelligence or machine learning) and applied linguistics. The purpose of making possible the computer-assisted understanding and processing of information expressed in human language for tasks such as chatbots or automatic translators.

Cognitive sciences

It aims to describe, explain, and imitate human thought and knowledge mechanisms. According to the Cervantes Institute, cognitive sciences are the meeting point between cognitive psychology and artificial intelligence, "Its objective is to study how people and machines assimilate new data, process it and act accordingly."

Conversational agent or chatbot

They are interactive dialogue systems that manage the interactions between man and machine through artificial intelligence. The interface can conduct a dialogue, ask questions, and provide answers according to predefined rules. In HR, the recruiting agents can use these virtual agents to interpret the language to collect information from the candidates, formulate selection questions and answer precise queries, which can be sent directly to the Applicant Tracking System (ATS).

Predictive analytics

It consists of applying statistics and methods of different artificial intelligence types to predict future events or the evolution of variables. It is based on the predictive hypothesis that several similar situations will experience the same development if this has been the past case. This type of artificial intelligence allows us to anticipate hiring at a given year according to the time and rate of rotation or even determine, within a group of candidates, who will be the most attractive candidates for your company in the future.

So how do all these elements come together?

AI combines machine learning, deep learning, and decision trees. Any AI can be supervised or unsupervised and uses algorithms and artificial intelligence types, such as neural networks based on deep learning. In this way, artificial intelligence systems such as chatbots or predictive analyses are based on data or big data.

In addition to this, there can be no authentic deep learning without big data.

However, we must recognize that data science is still in its infancy regarding recruiting and hiring. It is not yet the panacea that employers hope for. One of the challenges in this regard is that most data scientists know very little about the context of employment. Many of them build their models based on the attributes of the "best performers." This approach is a slippery slope because a failure to check for any real difference between high-performing and low-performing employees on these attributes restricts their usefulness. Another challenge is that gleaning data from social media or websites people have visited raises privacy issues. Besides, someone's posting on social media as an undergraduate student may impact their hiring algorithm many years later. This strategy seems unfair.

Only a few employers collect the large amount of data required. This approach negatively impinges on the ability of the algorithms to make accurate predictions.

Motivation

Fundamental to the understanding of perception is the problem of motivation. Generally, industrial conflict and cooperation grow out of the needs of individual human beings. Every industrial dispute has a background of conflict, tension, and hostility. In the long run, every management and labor union official who wants to reduce the frequency of conflict must consider workers' perceptions, goals, frustration, and aggression. Many industrial disputes may occur. Some of them may be avoidable. Management and labor unions must learn more about human emotions and thinking. A proper perception of persons, situations, and issues by management and employees' union will reduce tensions. Then, efforts can be directed constructively for organizational effectiveness, innovation in manufacturing, product development, quality, and technological enhancement.

Fostering a competitive spirit

In coordinating their people into a working team and a winning combination, a supervisor/manager can use some of the techniques that the famous American football coach Vince Lombardi used to motivate players in the Green Bay Packers team. This team attained great success when Vince Lombardi was the coach. Apart from his coaching skills, he was also a master motivator. His constant motivation, encouragement, and the spirit of excellence he inculcated in the players significantly influenced the team's success. He once said, "The quality of a person's life is in direct proportion to his or her commitment to excellence, regardless of the chosen field of endeavor." He meant that it does not matter what one does for a living. The critical question is whether they are committed to excellence. Whether a person is a coach or a supervisor, they must help people acquire the right mental attitude and the physical skills to win.

Supervisors' active and purposeful interface

In this context, the question is, what attitudes must a supervisor, like a coach, instill in their people to draw out their best performance? First, the supervisor must instill in them the desire to do a good job. Encouragement is a magical elixir that can motivate people and spur productivity. The desire to be recognized and made to feel important is a basic human desire. Therefore, most employees crave recognition and support. In other words, the hunger for high achievement must be triggered in the people. Once this powerful emotion is activated, it has the potential to become an unstoppable force. But the high achievement attained must be recognized and rewarded.

Setting achievable targets

If the supervisor sets high work standards, people will work hard to meet them. However, putting them too high will be counterproductive and defeat their purpose. People will strive hard to accomplish a goal if they believe they can. However, they may quickly lose enthusiasm when they do not achieve satisfying results despite their efforts. If one sets standards a little above subordinates' heads, they will reach down inside and come up with something they probably did not think they had. If they believe in their supervisor/manager, they will try. But if the expectations are too high, they may fail and feel frustrated and disappointed.

Encouraging personal goals

Supervisors/managers must encourage those reporting to them to set their goals. It is a fact that workers become more involved in their jobs when they participate in the goal-setting process. They should be encouraged to take pride in their performance.

Setting a good example

A supervisor's/manager's example will be the most powerful motivator. The supervisor/manager who insists that their team members be prompt and arrives late for work could be a better leader. Leading by example is very important. To bring out the best in others, one must show what level of performance is expected by one's actions. Coach Vince Lombardi never expected anything more of his players than he expected of himself. Leading by example is crucial as it can motivate the team to excel.

Being consistent

When a supervisor/manager sets a personal example, they must ensure consistency. In any organization, employees resent following orders that they think are arbitrary, capricious, or unreasonable. Employees want to predict how their boss will react to them and the problems that occur in the department. Maintaining consistent behavior takes practice, commitment, and self-confidence.

The supervisor/manager who feels burdened and frustrated by problems tends to react before considering a matter. They may suddenly lash out at subordinates, not because of anything they have done, but because they feel overwhelmed and unable to cope. If a supervisor/manager is unpredictable, their deputies will respond by being overly cautious and hesitant about making suggestions for improvement. This approach will eventually affect value creation.

Teaching fundamentals

Supervisors/managers must learn to observe their people from the sidelines so that their strengths and weaknesses can be detected and assessed with objectivity. If a worker is new, the supervisor must take the time to show them how to perform the tasks correctly. This strategy requires practice and commitment. If a subordinate needs to learn several techniques, taking them up one at a time would be preferable. Trying to teach a worker too many things initially will confuse and frustrate them.

Promoting team spirit

Whether in a company or on a football field, winning results are possible only through team spirit. If subordinates take pride in their work, believe in their supervisor/manager, and know they will be given reasonable goals, they will work together to achieve the desired objectives.

To avoid blocks or impediments to the team spirit, a supervisor/manager must treat all subordinates equally without showing any favoritism. Each person is unique and has needs that may differ from those of their fellow workers. A supervisor/manager must effectively appeal to each member of their team's unique needs. Only then can each team member work to their fullest potential and contribute equally to the team effort.

A supervisor/manager should provide tangible rewards to deserving team members whenever possible. Besides, team members greatly value the encouragement and praise from their supervisor/manager. Every employee wants to feel assured that their efforts will be rewarded. Therefore, supervisors/managers must give full credit for any cooperative behavior, innovative solutions to problems, or improvement in group performance. Sincere praise for actual accomplishment will lead team members to work together and accomplish tasks within the stipulated deadline.

When team members easily meet their goals, they should be provided with new plans to develop themselves to their fullest potential. In business, the department's total performance will tell the management how successful a coach is.

Employee Recognition

Employees crave respect and recognition. One of the core needs of all human beings is the desire to be treated with dignity. Therefore, treating all employees with respect is likely to result in multiple benefits. Employees treated with civility and respect by their supervisors/managers/mid-management executives/other leaders are likely to enjoy enhanced levels of health and well-being. They are expected to derive greater satisfaction and meaning from their jobs and have better focus and an improved ability to prioritize. They are also likely to stay longer with their organization. Therefore, corporate leaders who aspire to build a high-performance organization should be respectful to all employees. This approach will bring employee commitment and engagement, likely enhancing personal productivity.

Companies today are buffeted by the winds of change and the onslaught of global competition. Injecting more civility in the organization can help companies navigate today's uncertainty, turbulence, and volatility. Employees who feel they are being treated with dignity and respect are also much more motivated to embrace and propel change. Civility in an organization will also result in enhanced customer experience, adding value to the organization.

Mr. Robert McNamara, former chief of the World Bank, once said, "The proportion of inputs for success is one-third material and two-thirds the human factor. So, let us strive to develop the two-thirds first." Organizations must recognize this aspect of human resource management to improve their organizational effectiveness for growth and progress.

The identity of interests is the health, progress, and growth of the company they work for. Therefore, the workforce must appreciate that well-being is essential for continued employment and progression. At times, differences may arise and disturb this harmony. Action must be taken to iron out these differences in the shortest time possible. They can be resolved by democratic methods, namely discussions, persuasion, and education. Human resource is a very vital resource requiring the utmost attention. Organizational effectiveness is determined to a considerable extent by the management's ability to raise the workforce to the highest performance levels possible.

Further, uniformity and fairness must be practiced well in dealing with people to avoid conflicts and motivate them. Internal audit studies may be conducted on procedures covering recruitment, performance appraisals, promotions, and workforce planning. These studies could also combine tasks to make the job content more exciting and rewarding and identify potential persons for higher job responsibilities. Human resource management is a highly emotional and subjective task. The employees' union will search for unfair and unsafe operating practices to distort the employees' minds against the management. Therefore, it is necessary for a midlevel management team to periodically brief groups of employees on the company's fair and honest approach and promote excellent safety practices and environmental issues. To a large extent, this will curb distorted information that may lead to disturbances.

Today, industrial and commercial activity is engulfed in a maze of legislation in many parts of the world, including emerging markets in Asia/Africa and the European Union. Innumerable enactments and statutes govern various aspects of such activities. Many amendments to such legislation are made periodically. The scope and content of these legislations are pervasive and onerous. Compliance with these regulations, in many cases, rests with the senior management, namely, the board of directors and the CEO. A periodic audit of this aspect is necessary to ensure the company complies with various statutory provisions. Violating rules may lead to legal expenses, financial penalties, and other punitive measures.

Education and Employability

When qualified persons are recruited in today's changing circumstances, there is often a mismatch between their knowledge and industry needs. Undoubtedly, a diploma or degree will give some understanding of the subject. Working in an industry will expose them to the company's culture and work environment. Companies invest vast sums of capital in upgrading their technology and facilities. Academia may not have the requisite staff with exposure to modern technological advancements or lab facilities. In these circumstances, companies will have to have in-house programs to train the employees and help them acquire the requisite technical skills and other skills such as communication, group dynamics, teamwork, problem-solving, decision-making, and innovation. Therefore, in-house training facilities to upgrade jobs, knowledge, hands-on training, and skills would be beneficial. Besides, in-house training programs will likely be more relevant for the organization. The focus will be on imparting the specific skills that the company requires the employees to possess. Many multinational companies, such as McDonald's, have established corporate universities. In India, the Aditya Birla Group with strong presence in a diverse group of industries, has created an integrated world-class training center headed by a Chief Learning Officer. This state-of-the-art centralized training facility in Mumbai, India, provides a wide range of programs to cater to all their group companies' specific needs. The advantage of having an in-house training center or corporate university is that the training can be customized according the organizational needs. This will ensure that valuable time is not frittered away in acquiring skills that are not relevant for the company's needs.

Training and Development

The adoption of new technology calls for the development of complementary technical skills. Similarly, competitive pressures require improved systems, which again require additional capabilities. For instance, the need to process vast amounts of information, interpret data for effective managerial decision-making, and establish control systems for complex scheduling areas will require quantitative techniques and computerization knowledge. In a manufacturing company, there is a need to develop skills in operating and maintaining sophisticated machinery on the shop floor. For moving to the higher managerial levels, there is also the need to develop skills in working with people.

Programmed and systematic training is vital for achieving the desired goals. Coaching is a continuous lifelong process by which individuals can develop from learning basics to sophisticated professional skills. Training for the job is essential, and a person's ability to carry out a task will depend mainly on the quality of the training given.

Training can be broken down into several segments:

1. Induction
2. Apprentice or trainees
3. In-plant training
4. Refresher course
5. Continuing education

Training should be embedded into the corporate philosophy of any organization and cover all organization's tiers from the Chief

Executive down to the worker. Integrated training is essential for results.

While the needs of each organization are different, the experiences of companies who have been very successful in formulating and implementing innovative training programs can serve as a template for other companies that aspire to design such programs.

In this context, it will be interesting to note that some far-sighted companies in emerging countries have developed innovative training programs to compete effectively with their global competitors.

One such company is Ennore Foundries (now renamed Hinduja Foundries) in Chennai in the state of Tamil Nadu in Southern India. It is India's largest automotive jobbing foundry. When the co-author of this book served as Managing Director (MD), in-house training programs were meticulously developed at this company. The MD played a key role in the designing and implementation of these training programs. The training program was divided into two categories: (1) for managers and staff and (2) for the other employees. Under each category, a general and specialized training program was designed. The general training program included a more extended orientation session for recruits to develop group consciousness and to assist them in understanding the organization's corporate philosophy. This program was followed by other training programs on performing the required activities and another program to develop skills in different areas and subjects.

On advancement to a middle-level management career, employees were given training sessions to develop their analytical skills and foster a team approach to problem-solving. Upon reaching the Assistant Managers' level, a short-term training session was given to build their management capabilities. During their career as

Assistant Managers, they were exposed to programs that helped them enhance their problem-solving skills and improve their business judgment. Upon promotion as Managers, the program further enhanced the skills they had developed as Assistant Managers.

Specialized training programs included technical subjects, control procedures, digital technology, and people management. Technical training programs were divided into (1) elementary and (ii) applied. The duration of the program was different for elementary and applied training. Elementary training consisted of an introduction to technology and lessons on quality control. Applied training involved discussions on the application of specific techniques. Training on control procedures was divided into three parts - the first two were for a short duration on a study of control systems, applications of laid down work procedures and practices, application of statistics/data, and operations research. The third part of the training was regarding diagnostic skills and control techniques. Besides another training program was on the application of computers and digital technology.

From the above, one can appreciate the importance of training at all hierarchy levels to harness human power for organizational effectiveness. In addition, Ennore Foundries is proof that world-class training can be imparted in a company even in an emerging country. What is required to make this happen is the clarity of vision and commitment by the CEO/MD to make such training possible.

Succession Planning

Succession planning is an important HR function. Traditionally, this involves formulating the organization's process, designing the necessary tools, and training critical stakeholders on what needs to be done. Divisional managers or unit heads then initiate the process of identifying potential succession candidates for critical roles. Individualized development plans are then created for potential successors based on the candidate's current skills and the skill set they would need to function effectively in their new role.

Data analytics is now significantly transforming the process of succession planning. Algorithms sift through many years of succession data to identify the critical success factors for a particular role. The divisional managers or unit heads identify the top five internal candidates for a specific role based on the insights gained through this process. Customized career development plans for each candidate can then be formulated based on their skills/competencies.

Data analytics can also provide insights into employee personality traits, leadership styles, and work patterns. These valuable insights can be used to enhance customer service. This approach will ultimately lead to improved financial performance and value creation. These potential benefits can be realized only if the management is willing and able to "walk the talk" and invest significantly in analytic skills and capabilities. The returns on this investment can be attractive.

Any company aspiring to become a world leader in its field must make its operations more efficient and ensure excellent management of its human resources. This strategy requires continuous process improvement using data analytics and user-experience-focused service improvement. This approach also requires the willingness to consider geographically diverse sourcing of talent and the use of emerging automation technologies that simplify and improve many HR processes. Executives who wish to link their talent efforts to corporate value creation must supplement experience-based wisdom with analytically-driven insights.

Teamwork

Harmony and teamwork are essential for organizational effectiveness. There is a fundamental identity of interests among the employees. This identity of interest is the health, progress, and growth of the company where they are employed. The workforce must appreciate that the company's well-being is essential for continued employment and advancement. At times, differences may arise between the management and the workforce and disturb this harmony.

Any company's success depends on its employees' collective performance, who are employed to advance the company toward its goals. To achieve these goals, the inspired effort of the employees who have a personal interest in the fortunes of the company which employs them is only the effective option. Therefore, each employee must strive to excel in their sphere of activity. In this context, a proper appreciation and understanding of excellence are necessary. It is not about surpassing others. It is a question of excelling oneself in whatever one does. This approach is why it is a matter of one's attitude. The attitude to excel in one's performance and continuously strive to enrich oneself by experimenting, trying new ways and methods, and searching for new experiences. This attitude for striving and stretching oneself toward higher attainments comes about when one becomes aware that we can undertake any challenge and give out our very best to succeed and experience satisfaction. It will result in the joy of striving in the right direction. Here comes the human faculty's play of discrimination of selecting and striving for the right and higher values. When we accept the correct values and strive to live up to them, our weaknesses will be transformed into strengths. For attaining success in any field, the prerequisites are self-belief, self-esteem, conviction of purpose or the goal to be achieved, and perseverance. Once the belief of purpose is there, our entire physical, mental, and intellectual efforts will be directed toward achieving the goal, paving the way for success.

In social and organizational life, more than individuals' knowledge and skills, the spirit of cooperation and collaboration with which they work becomes crucial for the group's overall success and vital for the group or organization's overall success. An organization is not merely an assemblage of persons, so the organization succeeds with all persons' contributions. This approach should be more than the aggregate of individual contributions. This synergic effect will be there, provided people work together to inspire a shared vision, common goal, and personal dedication. Therefore, the members' mental and intellectual preparedness to become more sensitive to and aware of how they can help meet the group or organization's needs through what they do is more important than the mere "physical" team.

Industrial Relations

Good industrial relations are necessary for organizational success. The absence of industrial conflicts does not mean good industrial relations. Harmonious relationships must be worked out smoothly by the management and labor without allowing for the dramatic occurrence of strikes and lockouts. We need to know the sequences of events that lead to harmony or violence. We need to understand the forces that lead to action and reaction.

Today, "industrial relations" often refer to group interactivity with events involving the management and the labor union. Industrial conflict and industrial cooperation occur as immediate consequences of the action of individuals. The facts guide their actions as they are seen by the individuals concerned. These may be differences in perception between managers, employees, and union committee members. Agreement on specific facts provides a basis for cooperation. Disagreement often leads to conflict. Therefore, it is fundamental to understand the proper perception of a situation leading to a problem or motivation. Generally, industrial strife and cooperation grow out of the needs of individual human beings. Every industrial dispute has a background of conflict, tension, and hostility.

In the long run, management and labor union officials who want to reduce conflict frequency must consider the perceptions, goals, frustrations, and aggression of workers. Many industrial disputes may occur. Some of them may be avoidable. The management and labor union must learn more about human thinking and emotions. A proper perception of persons, situations, and issues by both management and labor will reduce tensions. Efforts can then be directed constructively for organizational effectiveness, innovation in manufacturing, product development, quality, and technological enhancement. The success of the Japanese companies is mainly due to people management and the commitment. of their workforce. Much practical wisdom and experience are available at all organizational levels. The key to organizational success lies in exploiting this potential to the fullest extent possible.

Generally, industrial conflict and cooperation grow out of the needs of individual human beings Usually, companies have standing orders that lay down the do's and don'ts of employees and the action to be taken where there is misconduct. The various wrongdoings are listed in the standing orders and the steps that would follow. Labor unions' tactic in emerging countries such as India, called "go slow," can also be construed as misconduct. Then, efforts can be directed constructively for organizational effectiveness, innovation in manufacturing, product development, quality, and technological enhancement.

A Case Study

Due to the socialist path that India took after its independence from Britain, labor unions have traditionally played a dominant role in Indian industry. The labor unions have historically been aggressive and local in voicing their demands. This fact, coupled with restrictive labor laws which limit the flexibility of the management to hire and fire personnel, have made it a very challenging environment for companies to operate in. Despite these challenges, some companies in India, led by visionary and empathic leaders, have managed to survive and prosper.

One such company is Ennore Foundries (now known as Hinduja Foundries). It is a large automotive mechanized jobbing foundry in the city of Chennai in the state of Tamil Nadu in South India. The co-author served as Managing Director of this company for many years. A review of the human resources practices at this company can provide useful insights that may be of value to the management at companies in emerging countries.

One of management's main foci was keeping employees happy at the workplace. It was sometimes about something other than remuneration. Many workers used to commute from a great distance to get to the foundry and had a long day at work. Therefore, management felt that the employees coming to work must be made to feel happy. This feeling would, in turn, improve their productivity and performance.

The management decided the focus should be on employees' aspirations, welfare, social status, growth opportunities, skill development, and overseas training. The management felt this would be the right approach to earn employees' cooperation and trust. The management also believed that this approach would build harmony and team spirit. All managers and supervisors were told to implement this corporate philosophy faithfully.

Some of the innovative ideas which were conceived and successfully implemented in this Foundry are given below:

1. Two-tier dearness allowance schemes (DA). One for routine work and the other to recognize full monthly attendance to reduce absenteeism. In addition, Management introduced a free breakfast scheme for employees. Dearness allowance is an extra compensation given to the employees as a reward, and as an incentive for productivity.
2. The DA scheme was modified to recognize the differential skills of various trades/occupations.
3. During a recession in the auto industry in India, it was vital to maintain the daily output at a high rate. Production could

not be made up by overtime due to the furnaces' cycle time limitations. The working week was compressed to three days in one week and four days in the next to optimize the use of scarce resources like electric power.

4. The "Go Slow" tactic used by the labor union to lower production was defined and included in the standing orders as willful misconduct.

5. a. "Responsibility award" for maintaining the delivery of castings at a minimum level monthly was instituted, with the reward paid quarterly.

   b. Scrap (wastage) reduction reward was also offered for maintaining and improving scrap percentage. This reward was paid on a half-yearly basis.

   c. Incentive schemes calculated on the performance of each day. It was either individual or small group based. This scheme was an adaptation of the Halsey Premium Plan and was based on the time saved (actual time–standard time) multiplied by their incentive rate

   d. The periodic incentive payments linked to performance were introduced to sustain the annual bonus.

6. A part of the "Responsibility Award," payable to workers, was contributed to the workforce's welfare fund. This fund was to meet employees abnormal medical expenses, merit scholarships for employees' children, funeral expenses, purchase of property for the employees union, or improve it. The Union brought some land in Tiruvottiyur (near Chennai, Tamil Nadu, India), and the management built a union building/Kalyana Mantapam (marriage venue) out of this initiative. The employees greatly appreciated this gesture by the management.

7. The objective of the free breakfast for employees' scheme was to ensure good health and regular attendance.

8. Good, subsidized lunch was also offered to all employees. These two gestures by the management reduced absenteeism and improved productivity.

9. A policy of promotions from within the organization, provided the employees had the required qualification and competence, was implemented.

10. Free transportation was provided for employees in the second shift ending at 12:30 AM when no public transport was available.

During the sweltering summer days, when working in the Foundry's hot environment was very uncomfortable, two weeks of compulsory annual vacation was given, excluding essential employees. The plant maintenance was scheduled then, and employees could spend this time with their families or do whatever they wanted. This strategy was beneficial to both employees and the company. This policy was also built into the standing orders of the company.

The management organized seminars and meetings periodically for workers and supervisory staff. These programs were designed to improve trust and confidence in the management and create a sense of belonging to the company. About one hundred to two hundred persons were chosen randomly for such meetings across all departments, with the CEO personally participating in these meetings. These programs were very well received. They generated a lot of enthusiasm and interest among the participants. A well-designed video showing the company's advancement was played at the start of the meetings to project the company's technical and environmental progress.

There were also discussions on the threats and the opportunities the company faced were also discussed at these meetings. The topics covered in these discussions included:

a. Quality
b. Changing customer needs
c. Importance of delivery of the goods on time
d. Customer is the king
e. Changes in technology and its implications for the company
f. Relevancy of dies/patterns/tooling accuracy
g. Perform or perish
h. Quality comes first
i. Customers are the focus of our efforts
j. Continuous improvement is essential in everything done or to be done
k. Repose trust in and depend on people
l. Must surpass competitors in overall performance
m. Employees' progress closely depends on the company's good health and viability
n. Reach out to employees to give the employees a correct perception of the organization's strategy for growth

Renowned speakers from NGOs were invited to topics of relevance to the employees. This was in addition to talks by renowned subject matter experts.

Much thought was given to designing the programs, and the managing director selected the faculty for these programs and the guest speakers. The faculty for such programs were drawn from within the company as well as from outside. The speakers included orators in the local language (Tamil) and distinguished professors from the prestigious Indian Institute of Technology, Madras, India. Eminent management consultants were also invited as guest speakers.

Many management development programs, seminars, and meetings covered changes and challenges before the company, were organized. These included the need for industrial harmony, winning customer confidence, satisfaction, cost, quality, productivity, and skills. These programs were designed to connect the workforce emotionally and for mass action to enhance performance so that major instructions could be converted into mass movements. An indirect outcome of such programs was an improvement in employee relations and a better appreciation of management goals, direction, progress, and wholehearted support of the employees for the company's stability and growth programs.

These distinctive and carefully designed programs helped build a harmonious relationship between the management and the labor union officials, and fellowship among employees who felt a sense of belonging and pride to be working for an organization that cared deeply about their welfare. . This strategy helped the company to successfully cope with many challenging situations and maintain its dominant and preeminent position in the automotive foundry in India.. It also helped to send a message to everyone in the company that they should work with a certain amount of extra diligence and zeal, carefully observing the procedures and methods for various operations. The employees were also sensitized to the fact that greater attention should be given to avoid wasting scarce resources such as electricity, raw materials, and time. Furthermore, supervisors had to be more vigilant to anticipate things that could go wrong and take prompt action to prevent it. This approach was based on the view that there is no room for complacency. All employees in the organization must be more vigilant to ensure that quality products reach customers on time and enhance customer experience.

Management had a philosophy of reaching out to its employees. Therefore, seminars were organized for operators annually to highlight the areas where their attention, involvement, and efforts were mainly required. The classification of executives under different grades was made scientifically. Designations were changed in line with their grading, giving them a better status inside and outside the company. The compensation package was also liberalized. Management introduced several welfare measures. Encouragement was given to employees to acquire additional qualifications. Actions were initiated to draw on the experience and knowledge of the employees to improve production and productivity. The chief executive and a specially designated team designed training programs for all executives on management, quality, and cost improvement concepts. Management conferences were also held for senior executives and managers to draw up the plans for the year and review them in the middle and end of the year. Another feature that was successfully tried out was that persons who were sent out for training programs or seminars, had to address a group of persons who had not had the opportunity to participate in such programs. One more idea successfully tried out was sending office staff to the factory on night shifts to appreciate and understand the factory environment's intricacies and conditions. The CEO participated in training programs and addressed employees. His inspiring and motivational speeches were very well received by the employees and helped to build team spirit.

The Foundry collaborated with the premier Indian Institute of Technology, Madras, India, for technical and management development programs. This strategy was an example of academia-industry collaboration.

Choosing the correct type of motivation to inspire employees resulted in spectacular results and a deep sense of fulfillment. When all aspects of one's personality are geared toward determined goals, we can overcome obstacles with the total personality's strength and achieve the chosen goals. Therefore, an innovative approach to dealing with employees individually and as a group is essential and a sine qua non for organizational success..

In line with the company's philosophy of "reaching out" to its employees, seminars for operators were organized every year to highlight the areas where their attention, involvement, and efforts were required. The classification of executives under different grades was made scientifically. Designations were changed in line with their grading to give them a better status inside and outside the company. The compensation package was also liberalized. Several welfare measures were introduced. Encouragement was given to employees to acquire additional qualifications. Actions were initiated to improve production and productivity by drawing on the employees' experience, knowledge, and suggestions. Training programs for all executives on management concepts, quality cost improvement, and process technology were designed. Management conferences were also held for senior executives and managers to draw up the plans for the year and review them in the middle and at the end of the year.

The human resource management practices at Ennore Foundries can serve as a template for manufacturing companies in emerging countries that have to operate in a challenging, resource constrained environment. Instead of viewing constraints as impediments to success, they can be seen as an opportunity to design creative solutions that will lead the company to success.

Technology

For any country to be self-reliant, the most cost-effective processes and new technologies must be accorded priority. This is especially true for emerging countries that are trying to establish themselves in the global economy. The need for companies in emerging markets is to revamp the production base with updated technology, and adapting it to specific needs. Modernizing existing technologies may reduce employment opportunities. If the cost of preserving employment results in poor performance and financial distress, perpetually tolerating it as a social obligation is unjustified. Unfortunately, in many emerging countries, the governments exert a lot of pressure on companies to comply with the government's social agenda, even though it may be detrimental to the companies' financial health. With the increasing complexities of global business and supply chain challenges caused by geopolitical challenges, the choice of buying and adapting technologies has become a very complex issue. Companies must put in place systems for the objective evaluation and the cost-benefit analysis of modern/new technology acquisition.

The adoption of new technology does not guarantee commercial success. Its impact is on the overall organization, not merely the technical aspects. Resolving the technical issues is relatively easy— new machines can be installed, a unique manufacturing process instituted, and new R&D facilities established. These are necessary and important, but looking at the far more complex organizational processes and human issues involved is essential to make them fully effective. In the final analysis, the human resource and the strategies centered around it will transform the new technology into sustained profitability and growth. This will result in value creation.

Technology is at the core of innovation. Technology and innovation are two sides of the same coin; one cannot exist without the other. But the essential prerequisite for a technological society is innovation. The reason why innovation is so much more important than capital is that innovation also improves profits. A crucial difference between a technology-based society and a traditional one lies in the industry's contribution to the quality of human resource development.

Manufacturing

Production systems employed today to by manufacturing companies even in emerging countries to produce high quality products, have shifted from a labor-intensive to a knowledge-intensive pattern due to rapid technological advances and widespread industrial robot adoption in production lines and other advanced technologies. The engineers' and others' educational backgrounds must be successfully tapped to stimulate and upgrade manufacturing techniques. Further, direct attention will have to be paid to other new areas such as digitization, water management, air quality engineering, heat recovery systems, new materials, composites, space management technology, waste management, waste recycling, and industrial engineering. These are significant areas for manufacturing companies to focus efforts on.

For many years, companies in many emerging countries were operating under a sheltered environment. So, there was no incentive to adopt the latest technologies and manufacturing processes. For instance, during the pre-liberalization era in India, businesses operated in a sellers' market in a sheltered environment with government protection from competition. Therefore, there was no technological enhancement in these circumstances, no thrust for R & D efforts for product development, and poor after-sales service. The markets tolerated inefficiency, low quality, and the absence of alternatives. Industry seldom worried about quality, innovation, and upgrading of technology. But once countries such as India, discarded the shackles of a socialist economic environment and embraced the market economy, companies in these countries were exposed to the onslaught of global competition. These companies realized that, in order to compete effectively on the global stage, they had to quickly adopt the latest technologies and business practices or go out of business. They realized that they had to either adapt or die. Therefore, there was a realization that an attitudinal change, and openness, are required to be daringly different and compete effectively.

Finding ways to do things better, break the monotony, and improve curiosity while working with the enormous knowledge, wisdom, and tools available now are essential to gain new experiences. Learning must be built into all aspects of the business or organization. Employees must feel comfortable making suggestions, taking risks, experimenting with new ideas, and giving and receiving free and frank feedback. Teamwork and a collaborative approach must be encouraged to produce better results. The pooling of cross-disciplinary expertise and wisdom skills is required. It must be developed for effective teamwork if people do not have it. The buck stops with the CEO. Therefore, the CEO is ultimately responsible for the handling of all feedback information - customer complaints, employees' grievances or aspirations, suggestions, and safety concerns.

All plant and machinery to be purchased must be considered part of a whole manufacturing system, not individual equipment or hardware. This strategy ensures balanced and cohesive output from all the individual machines.

Economic liberalization in many developing countries, such as India, has brought about a sudden change in the business environment. New technology has been inducted in all sectors; competition has become sharper; customers' demands have become more exacting, and consumers have alternatives. Organizations, therefore, will have to equip themselves to meet this new situation intelligently by effectively inducting the latest technology, plant, and equipment, testing and measuring instruments, skilled and knowledgeable workforce, adopting innovative techniques, and striving for high morale of the employees to ensure excellence in operations. Performance, productivity, and growth in an organization will depend, to a large extent, on the style and quality of leadership at every level of hierarchy in the organization.

To select plant & machinery, and technology, deep thought and careful evaluation are required. A technology audit may be done to identify gaps in the existing technology. The technology must be capable of easy assimilation by local labor. Wherever it is possible, the overseas plant suppliers must be persuaded to use components or computer systems of manufacturers who operate in a country where the machine is to be installed and used. In other words, choosing a foreign supplier with a base in the country of use would be better.

Further, research could be done worldwide for the latest plant and equipment working successfully with minimal downtime, process waste, and consistency in manufactured products. In this exercise, involving premier educational Institutions such as IIT (Indian Institute of Technology) in India will be very helpful. Such institutions exist in other emerging countries as well. A collaboration, which can be mutually beneficial, should be initiated with such institutions. The technology chosen should be updated quickly. The Import Trade Control regulations, if any, must be carefully studied to reduce the impact on the overall cost. The space required for the plant vis-à-vis its effect on the civil engineering cost must also be carefully examined. Working from outside the factory, the outsourcing effect encourages senior retired employees to set up their units with the company's support to buy the products made, which must be nurtured and considered.

Finally, the choice should be for:

1. Best equipment adopted worldwide with easy, reliable, and timely access to spare parts
2. Equipment capable of producing products with consistency in quality
3. Best practices and technology in manufacturing capable of easy assimilation
4. Delivery of the plant within the shortest time possible
5. Insured CIF at the installation/usage destination of the plant
6. Excellent pollution control and safety measures

Innovation

Innovation does not only mean discovering or inventing something new. The mental faculties' direction is to explore the possibilities to see if the work can be done better/more safely and with reduced process time. The approach should be for continuous improvement. This approach will stimulate the thinking process of the employees and make their work more interesting.

To compete effectively, companies have realized the importance of innovation. Therefore, CEOs pay closer attention to their corporate R & D departments' functioning because they are the fulcrum that fosters innovation and enhances competitiveness. CEOs need to build a corporate culture that embraces new technologies, triggers the passion for knowledge, and reduces (and eventually eliminates) barriers to creativity.

A CEO who aspires to build an agile, innovative organization must anchor creative individuals in critical roles and task them for overseeing accountability for the organization's objectives, essential focus areas, core competencies, and commitments to all stakeholders. The CEO should empower such people by giving them the latitude and discretion to conduct their work within this framework. Employees should also be encouraged to interact with their colleagues in the internal innovation chain.

The biggest impediment to innovation is a bureaucratic, sclerotic, and hierarchical organizational structure. Such a system can stifle creativity and demotivate talented employees. Therefore, the CEO and top management should create channels allowing innovative individuals to bypass the hierarchical structure. Employees at all levels with innovative ideas should be encouraged to bring them to top management's attention. When talented and creative individuals in the organization feel that the top management respects them and that their views are given due consideration, they will be motivated to strive for the organization's betterment. Employees should be encouraged to put forth seemingly impractical ideas because such ideas may trigger a discussion that could lead to exciting new possibilities.

Ensuring that creative, innovative individuals do not overextend themselves by getting involved in too many projects is vital. A maximum of two projects at any given time would be ideal.

The top management should be open to bringing in external teams to work with the innovative in-house teams. Such collaboration could be very useful in developing and commercializing new technologies.

R and D leaders in an organization need to step away from hiring individuals who prefer to work in silos. Instead, they need to hire people who would be flexible and willing to join multiple projects. They should also be allowed to move from one task to another as needed. This approach would help broaden the repertoire of skills of these individuals.

Innovation is an essential factor in high performance. This view does not mean that traditional methods should be given up and that everything must be done differently. It is the development of an attitude of mind to think whether a job could be done better, whether a job can be done safely, whether it could be done faster or cheaper, and so on. In tapping creative abilities, it is necessary to clear all barriers to creative thinking. One's power of analysis or perceptiveness determines one's ability to visualize new concepts. A questioning approach is vital to the creative process. The creative process's most significant catalyst is the question "why," and a close runner-up is the question "why not." Both questions stimulate creative thought. Acute powers of observation will supply the working material for creativity. Observation powers must be active, accurate, and capable of scanning various options. No laid-down formula exists to direct creative thought. An individual action plan must be developed. Innovation offers an extraordinary and scarcely realized potential for further development. Suppose we will claim, for example, that casting is a unique production engineering process. In that case, there must be far more innovation in production engineering, control, and product development. In this context, in-house R & D activity and effort should be emphasized.

Product Development

Managers should "think first" by careful planning in the very design of the product. Before a design is finalized, detailed discussions must occur between engineering, production, quality assurance, and marketing personnel. Manufacturing and industrial engineers should help determine specifications, methods, and standards. The product design should be viewed as part of a total product-process system.

The primary function of management is planning. Some authorities say that the secret of the Japanese success after World War II was the methodical practices of people, leaving little to chance. Today's skills, processes, and facilities may be inadequate as markets shift and competition strengthens. Detailed and intelligent planning is vital for successfully meeting future challenges.

Planning is a process of making decisions today with the future in mind. Planning is merely deciding today what should be done for tomorrow to achieve the desired goals. In business, it involves reconciling scarce resources such as money, personnel, equipment, or skills with the long-term objectives and opportunities or threats that may arise. Good planning helps organizations to monitor and achieve better performance and improved efficiency. Here, we are reminded of a very relevant maxim. "If you fail to plan, you plan to fail."

Planning and Managerial Efficiency

With extensive investments in plant and equipment and increased labor costs, the breakeven point moves higher and necessitates high-capacity utilization levels. Time lost due to breakdowns and industrial disputes must be minimal. All machines must be operated to full capacity. The output of all machines should be in balance. The better the capacity utilization, the higher the margins, and with lower utilization, the fall in margins is very steep. A high degree of concentration is required to achieve daily targeted production. Constant watch is necessary to ensure it does not drop due to power failure and voltage fluctuation. Inter-departmental coordination and employee involvement will be beneficial for this purpose. A higher degree and a better appreciation of the interdependency of the company's various functional areas is vital for success.

The growth pattern for the next five years must be visualized. The products manufactured may undergo a substantial change. Customers' requirements for quality and timely delivery may become more exacting. Reduction in power supply, called "power cuts" in emerging countries such as India, imposed by the electricity provider may continue, requiring consideration for in-house generating capacity. New products with overseas collaboration will likely enter the market significantly, creating new growth opportunities. Therefore, a multi-pronged approach would be necessary to meet these diversified challenges. This strategy would include enhancing technology and process, in-house electricity generation facilities, and training programs for all tiers of employees in the company in the changing environment. New techniques, information dispersal, computer applications, organizational changes, strengthening marketing, R & D, machine building, design, and development must be treated simultaneously for overall corporate growth that will eventually lead to value creation.

Productivity

Productivity is the primary goal of all organizations. It is crucial for the survival of an organization. Hence, managements attempt to reach optimum productivity by using various financial and non-financial incentives, changing styles/methods to more democratic and participatory techniques, or both, and sometimes using other tactics.

Productivity advances must be the primary source of raising real compensation for labor and their standard of living. It can be an effective anti-inflationary measure, but it can produce a cushion to increasing wage rates and other inputs' prices. The upward trend in productivity increases the competitive edge of indigenous products in international markets, ensures higher profits at the individual company level, and results in an overall increase in the country's GDP.

The productivity concept has its roots in "productivity function." Any organization's output volume depends on the quantities of labor and other inputs employed in production and the effective utilization of these inputs. Most organizations today operate in a resource-constrained environment. Therefore, corporations' challenge is optimizing and deploying available resources effectively to gain a competitive advantage.

Productivity is no longer an elusive concept. It means getting more and better output from a given input. Yet, economic planning continues to be obsessed with mere investments and growth rates, and there is undue emphasis on capital, often neglecting other factors.

Among all developing countries, India's productivity message has a special meaning, where scarcity of resources is the main hurdle for growth. This situation has resulted in the creative use of resources and constraint optimization. Low income meant low savings potential, which had led to inadequate capital formation. This conundrum held back production and income levels, thus resulting in a vicious cycle. Companies in developing countries are ahead in aspirations but need to catch up in terms of resources. Therefore, the importance and urgency of making the best use of limited resources such as electricity, water, raw materials, capital, and labor force and avoiding waste or under-utilization of installed capacity. India today has gained a reputation for frugal engineering. This is evidenced by its successful missions to Mars and the Moon. These were the lowest cost missions to these celestial bodies. The paucity of resources forced Indian scientists to think of creative ways to optimize the available resources while achieving the objectives on schedule.

The term productivity connotes different meanings to experts from various disciplines. To macroeconomists, it is an index aggregated at the level of the economy as a whole. To macroeconomists and macro-oriented management theorists, productivity is specific to industrial firms and organizations. On the other hand, organizational psychologists tend to focus on the productivity of individuals and small groups, assuming that increases in these units' performance will enhance the organization's performance.

Productivity plays a critical role in the economic development of a country. In the past, in developing countries such as India, the tradition was to patronize the decentralized economy (SMEs) and discourage better production methods, lest they increase unemployment. Avoiding an increase in unemployment was considered to be of paramount importance. But this desire to avoid increase in unemployment, that had its roots in the socialist mindset of the politicians during that period, came at a huge cost. Using outdated and inefficient means of production stymied progress and resulted in a stagnant economy. Companies were also shackled by socialist policies that discouraged private enterprises in India and other developing countries in the early years of the post-independence period.

Industrial engineers and behavioral scientists have studied productivity for a considerable time. Initially, greater emphasis was placed on machinery because productivity was considered synonymous with machine outputs. The human element was considered an appendage to the machine. Gradually, with the introduction of labor laws, there was a shift in emphasis. It is now recognized that the human element is also as important as an ingredient in organizational effectiveness and that no output is possible without the willing cooperation of this human element. Machines are now designed to suit and adjust to the operator's requirements. In general, the outcome of the interaction between performance and satisfaction is productivity. It is a fact that employees reach higher productivity levels when their energies are directed toward a higher purpose. In this regard, the management must "walk the talk to maintain credibility and build trust. An amalgamation of urgency, agility, capability, and corporate identity will help build a high-performance organization.

Quality

Managers should fundamentally recognize that quality is the key to survival. They should think of quality at every stage in designing the product, selecting the production process, and most carefully choosing suitable materials and inducting them. Detailed specifications for all incoming materials must be drawn up and updated periodically. Intensive effort should be directed to screening the incoming materials and giving the results to the suppliers. Pressure must be put on the suppliers to improve the quality of their materials. It will be desirable to work with the suppliers to ascertain why problems arise and solve them. Today, Japanese, Korean, and Chinese products have a worldwide reputation for precision, reliability, and durability. They have achieved this through hard work for an extended period. A multifold increase in profitability usually accompanies a slight reduction in defects. Fewer imperfections mean more output without a corresponding increase in cost. If you eliminate defective product production, things will become more straightforward and less costly. Rework can thus be avoided. Waste will go down. Inventory can be reduced. Above all, morale will go up high. Credibility will improve. Everyone in the organization would feel proud when only perfect products are produced. To succeed in business, companies must attain quality to match international standards, preventing waste and scrap products.

Once production begins, effort should be directed toward holding to these standards. Again, managers should ""think quality in" by training workers to deliver consistent, high-quality products. The production workers must automatically check the parts and components they receive to ensure they are defect-free. They should work meticulously, knowing that any defect arising from their laxity in operations will be spotted and embarrassingly traced back to them.

When the system works well, high-quality products become a source of pride for all employees. Therefore, efforts should always be on to reinforce this feeling continually.

Industrial establishments all over the world strive to achieve profitable growth. Increasing the production of goods and services can help achieve the goal of achieving profitable growth. Many people can increase production by working to improve the volume or increase productivity. Productivity can be achieved by optimum utilization of personnel, machinery, and mechanization of its operations where necessary, backed up by efficient planning and control at all stages of manufacture. The most pressing problem is not evolving better methods of increasing production but improving and sustaining quality by reducing defective products. High-quality attainment can reduce the cost of manufacture for both the manufacturer and user of the products. This strategy would also avoid claims for product liability. It will improve credibility as a supplier and attract more custom/customers.

Our customers are the final judges of our products, judging us by the products we manufacture and sell. Therefore, it is necessary to ascertain customers' quality requirements on a regular basis and understand their inspection and control procedures. The products of many of our major customers must conform to international quality standards. Therefore, improving the quality standards to meet the stringent quality requirements of sophisticated overseas customers is essential and is a strategic imperative. The continuous endeavor must be to reduce manufacturing costs by efficiently and economically utilizing scarce resources to provide customers with satisfaction and confidence. So, it would be prudent to review the approach to quality control methods periodically.

Let us now take the case of automobile foundries in developing countries. With substantial underutilization of installed capacity, the foundries in many developing countries such as India, it is necessary to prioritize quality and scrap(wastage) reduction for survival and growth. Quality control has two aspects: first, the manufacturing process controls and tests that aid production: second, inspection—the operation by which all quality control checks are evaluated.

The primary responsibility of production is to produce products to the required standards. Production personnel are assisted by personnel in other sections such as purchase, inspection, maintenance, personnel, finance, and industrial engineering to build quality into a product. This strategy is backed up efficiently by codifying process procedures systems in writing,

For achieving successful results in improving the quality of the output, the development of specific skills is essential:

a. development of an attitude of mind to analyze what is wrong.
b. Keen observation on the shop floor to detect deviations from methods and practices.
c. Skill in interpreting the quality control data to help set priorities and determine corrective action.
d. Besides the above, good housekeeping and strict discipline in observing the prescribed methods and processes will contribute substantially to quality improvement.

A few random management decisions will not achieve high quality. A complex, all-encompassing interactive management system with the uncompromising long-term support of top management can only achieve it. The basis of this system is more than merely an appropriate arrangement of people and machines. It is a way of thinking. We have heard the common saying, "You don't inspect the quality of a product. You have to build it in." The Japanese have gone a step further. Before you build it in, you must "think it in."

For any industrial establishment's growth, its products must conform to the highest dependability and durability standards. This approach implies the optimum utilization of available resources to produce quality goods and services at reasonable prices. One factor that assumes great significance in achieving this objective is controlling products at every manufacturing stage to ensure quality. product quality, appearance, life, reliability, and safety enter an individual's activity or industrial concern. It assumes particular importance in exporting products to ensure their acceptance against stiff global competition. Therefore, the need for the establishment of proper management control systems is essential.

The scenario in India and many other developing countries that are snowballing is intense competition among manufacturers. Considerable value engineering exercises are being carried out to reduce production costs and make products more competitive. Further, extreme scarcity and constraints may prevail concerning materials and power. The increased cost of materials, energy, labor, and environmental controls broadly impact companies' operations. There is a limitation on the extent of obtaining price increases from customers for cost escalation. It is a matter of concern that there has been a substantial decline in many companies' profitability over the last few years. In this context, improving quality by reducing defective products improves margins. A systems approach to quality management will go a long way in sustaining and enhancing quality.

Operating a manufacturing company in a developing country such as India, is a challenging task. Government policies could change when a new political party forms the government. Companies have to contend with vagaries in power supply and availability of raw materials. Therefore, despite the best efforts of the management, there are bound to be some shortcomings in the manufacturing process. For instance, the quality of raw materials may not always be consistent; dies and equipment might have worn out; workers' skills, application, and dependability may differ; gauges; calipers; balances; and other measurement instruments might have lost their accuracy. All these variables, whether by chance or some assignable cause, affect the quality of the finished product. Therefore, developing quality control measures to minimize losses due to substandard quality is essential.

Therefore, the development of a quality control system assumes importance. Such a quality control system's primary objective should be preventing defects rather than screening good products from inferior ones.

For an effective quality system, the following these primary quality objectives must be realized:

1. Achieve, maintain, and improve the needed quality of the product in a manner that will meet the customers stated or implied requirements in the most cost-effective manner possible.
2. Provide internal evidence that the quality intended is being achieved.
3. Assure the customer that the final product will meet the desired quality standards.
4. Intelligent interpretation of quality control information for setting priorities and determining corrective action.
5. Application of knowledge and experience to correctly diagnose defects for appropriate remedy.
6. Development of a proper attitude to analyze what is wrong rather than who is wrong.
7. Good housekeeping
8. Keeping abreast of the customer's quality parameters and enhancing their facilities to improve/ensure quality.

Work instructions should form the base of any written quality system. They are "How to do it" and "What results should be obtained." A quality system is a team effort and needs the workforce's involvement and cooperation. Quality is an attitude of mind. Consistency in the quality system is a team effort and requires workforce participation. Consistency in the quality of castings relies on people, their attitudes and awareness, and their ability to follow the laid-down systems in a disciplined manner. Any organization's future prosperity will depend upon how much it can offer/guarantee its customers' components/products of consistent quality and specification, including dimensional tolerance, microstructure, and mechanical properties. Supplying components or products of consistent quality will gain third-party accreditation and maintain viability and profitability. Maintaining quality in operations should be a strong motivator for most employees to ensure job security. It will increase customer confidence leading to increased or repeat orders, fewer customer audits and less surveillance, and willingness on the customer's part to place orders requiring more stringent quality standards, opening up new markets.

The most pressing problem for manufacturing companies is not increasing the number of production methods but improving quality and reducing defective products. The attainment of quality standards can reduce the manufacturing cost for both the manufacturer and the product's user. Our customers are the final assessors of our products, judging us by the quality of the products we manufacture and sell. It is necessary to periodically ascertain customer quality requirements and inspection and quality control procedure trends. Many of our major customers' products must conform to international quality standards. Therefore, to give customer satisfaction and confidence, and meet their expectations, it is essential to produce products of very high quality while reducing manufacturing costs, and conserving scarce resources.. It will be prudent for all organizations to periodically review their quality control approach and prioritize quality and total quality control.

There are two facets of total quality control: (1) Controls in the manufacturing processes and tests that aid production, (2) Inspection—the operation by which the result of all quality control checks is evaluated. Deliberate action has to be directed toward the following aspects for achieving quality: dimension; soundness; physical and mechanical properties; surface finish and cleanliness; chemical composition; microstructure; weight and density. Further, developing specific skills is essential for achieving successful results in improving the output's quality.

a. It is vital to develop an attitude of mind to analyze what is wrong rather than who is wrong.
b. Keen observation in the factory will assist in detecting deviations from laid down methods and practices.
c. Skill in interpreting the quality control data will help set up priorities and determine corrective actions.
d. Besides the above, good housekeeping and strict discipline in observing the prescribed methods and processes will contribute substantially to quality improvement.

Consistency and reliable quality will have to be the watchwords. Quality consciousness should permeate all levels in the organization. Quality is the responsibility of every person working in an organization. Faced with intense global competition, the only way a company can survive and prosper is by offering customers the highest quality products that incorporate the latest technology.

The key to the success of the Japanese in the field of manufacturing was competitive performance. They were able to bring into sharp focus the needs of the customers worldwide and satisfy them. The significant factors for their success were (a) clarity in identifying customer needs, (b) technology, (c) right quality products, (d) competitive prices, (e) quick response to changes, and (f) effective utilization of workforce.

Government, employers, and employees believe they will have to depend on exports to a large extent for their economic survival. The cooperation between the employer, government, industry, trade, and employees made this transformation possible in Japan. Their ability to produce quality goods at a low price enabled them to penetrate, in a big way, the international market and has placed them on a sound economic base. Raw materials are very scarce in the country; right from childhood, Japanese are taught not to waste resources but to conserve them effectively. They have, therefore, developed a culture and attitude of mind for preventing waste and recycling it. Their labor productivity is exceptionally high. The laborers in Japan have realized that they will lose business unless they can produce the day's output as planned and directed by the employer to meet the customers' needs. While they work, they continuously apply their minds to work simplification and increase productivity without sacrificing quality. They also attend to three or four machines simultaneously to improve productivity and break the monotony. They have successfully implemented the "just-in-time" concept in manufacturing and supplies.

Further, in their efforts to increase productivity, they firmly believe in "zero defect" in their manufacturing activities. Their defects are calculated as so many numbers per million rather than as a percentage, as is usually done elsewhere. They realize that a few customers who get defective products will likely spread dissatisfaction among the community, reducing business opportunities. The workers in Japan have rightly realized that their own and the country's economic prosperity depended entirely on the company's good health. Therefore, all their efforts are directed toward the financial viability of the company that employs them to ensure their prosperity, continuity of employment, and welfare activities.

Detailed and innovative planning based on scientific industrial engineering knowledge is required. Effectively monitoring the said plan will improve the situation and considerably reduce variances. This approach will also bring down process inventory. It will make available costly factory space for other useful purposes besides releasing scarce cash and reducing interest charges.

It is a myth to say that labor costs are cheap in India or other less developed countries. Labor cost in the organized sectors in most countries has become prohibitive. With the revision in operatives' wages periodically, say every three years, companies may become uncompetitive in the long run unless labor productivity is improved substantially to reduce production costs. Tight control of the headcount and a constant dialogue with the employees to impress upon them the necessity for enhancing labor productivity is essential. Team briefing, training programs, effective communication, and industrial engineering application are all necessary for achieving it.

Nuances of Financial Strategy and Reporting

Managers employ various systems to move information around the organization, make decisions, and implement changes. Planning and control systems are the most powerful tools for determining how organizations should work and what they want to accomplish. Financial control systems and planning control systems together give coherence and direction to the organization. Internal controls help in the successful accomplishment of the results. The efficacy of the management is quantifiable. It could be measured by the profit and loss account (income statement). We should use intelligence, knowledge, experience, and numbers to achieve results. No organization can run successfully without a razor-sharp focus on critical numbers. Numbers serve as a thermometer that measures the health and well-being of the enterprise.

For instance, numbers, as reflected in ratios, can serve as a handy diagnostic tool that can be used to assess the financial health of the company and understand its strengths and weaknesses. Well-managed companies pay a greater degree of attention to numbers. However, ratios, for instance, are only meaningful with a basis for comparison. Insightful inferences can be obtained through trend analysis, best-achieved results, industry comparison, and peer group comparison. In making up the budget for a year, we need to put a series of expectations/goals on paper expressed in numbers. They include the whole gamut of costs, anticipated income from sales, and return on investment. They are based on the best facts or other information available. The year's budget is a plan for the company. It lays down month-by-month projections for production, sales, profits, inventory, accounts receivable, workforce requirements, scrap (production waste) targets (in the case of a Foundry), and capital investments. As the budget year proceeds, the numbers reflecting the actual operations start pouring in. Production, sales, scrap, profit margins, loss, and earnings can be compared to budget forecasts. Such comparisons reveal whether one set of numbers matches the other and whether the actuals are above or below the company's expectations.

Any significant variation is a signal for corrective action. The numbers themselves will not tell us what to do. The critical issue is to find out what is happening behind those numbers. They must be read, understood, and interpreted intelligently. What should be sought is a comprehension of numbers and their meaning. That will come only with regular exposure, constant repetition, retention of what you have read in the past, and familiarity with the actual activities that the numbers represent. Gradually, you will feel at ease with numbers and their meaning. Numbers are your controls. Understanding numbers will give you greater confidence that you are in control and aware of the expected significant variations. Once you start delving into the areas that numbers represent, you will find the source of the problem for taking appropriate action. In short, you will be able to manage better with numbers. Better management of numbers and timely corrective action, when needed, will ultimately result in value creation.

It is advisable to prepare a five-year rolling plan. It may be designed, implemented, and updated every year after considering the previous year's performance and conducting a realistic future appraisal. It should set out the company's objectives and the direction in which the company should upgrade its manufacturing and other facilities to exploit emerging business opportunities. The goals are achievable with concentrated and coordinated efforts to improve the bottom-line figures. As projected, the margins must be achieved to generate the necessary cash flow to finance the capital expenditure programs. In addition, there must be an evaluation of whether the company's capital structure is compatible with the type of business that it is in. This approach will give comfort, and much confidence to the board of directors and investors, in operations and management. The first year of the five-year plan is the budget year.

In short, you will be able to manage better with the numbers. Every activity has two dimensions - physical and financial. While evaluating the efficacy of alternative approaches to solving a specific problem, executives should express the benefits of the chosen method in physical and financial terms, like its actual impact in improving the company's results.

The financial reporting may be based on the following format:

- Actual for each month and forecast for the year as the year progresses
- Budget for each month for comparing the actual performance
- Last year's actual performance

This format can be used for sales, profit, debtors, creditors, and scrap (production waste) (in the case of a foundry).

In this context, executives must have a clearer understanding of the business environment of their company. There are many challenges that executives must grapple with. The demand for stringency in quality is exacting. Competition is growing. The costs of all inputs are spiraling. The customers usually resist price increases. The critical question that arises in this context is: "How can the declining trend in the profitability of the operations be reversed?" Executives will have to find ways and means of increasing the efficiency of all the operations of the company. This approach could be through the economical buying of raw materials, cost-effective manufacturing processes, effective maintenance, and upkeep of all production and other related facilities. Besides rigorous quality checks, carrying a minimum inventory of materials work-in-progress and finished products through imaginative production planning and cost improvement programs would be very beneficial.

Cost improvement programs are not a one-time affair. They have to be a continuous and ongoing activity. In addition to improving margins, the quality of the product, and beating the competition, these programs will help develop specific skills and virtues essential for an individual's professional growth. It will sharpen the intellect, stimulate innovative thinking, develop leadership skills, encourage working together, and above all, give employees immense satisfaction that they have managed the resources entrusted to them efficiently. In short, the organization will become more efficient and profitable.

Suppose this vision of improving efficiency is to be turned into reality. In that case, considerable effort, determination, and attitudinal changes are required from everyone in the organization to improve margins that may be getting eroded. Many companies, especially in the Western World, have been making organizational changes, marketing innovations, and reducing production costs. Challenges are not confined to companies in the developing world. They impact organizations globally. Therefore, regardless of location, companies must strive to improve their margins for stability, growth, and value creation.

There are some fundamental ways to increase margins:

1. Reduce fixed overheads and variable costs of the business.
2. Increase sales volume
3. Raise the selling price
4. Launch cost reduction programs

5. Improve operational efficiency, improve installed capacity utilization, reduce plant downtime, control, and minimize rejections.

If the markets served are stagnant over time, increasing volumes may not be that easy, nor does not allow for an increase in the selling price. Reducing costs is, therefore, a logical and primary step. A low return on investment will not enthuse shareholders to invest more funds in the company. Therefore, it is in the interest of all concerned; the highest priority and importance should be given to reducing production costs and improving margins.

Some areas that deserve specific attention are:

1. Improving the productivity of capital
2. Cost of capital and interest charges
3. Composition of capital
4. Enhancing the productivity of labor
5. Anticipating what can go wrong and taking adequate measures to avert any crisis
6. Efficient working capital management, with particular emphasis on accounts receivable and inventories
7. Intelligently work out the debt-equity mix (the capital structure) that will be most appropriate for a company, given the nature of its business
8. Studies and research must be conducted on organizations in the same industry and other sectors to help determine the optimal debt-equity mix
9. Improved production planning to meet customers' schedules and avoid stagnation of inventory on the shop floor
10. More aggressive selling
11. More judicious purchasing
12. Better utilization of materials

13. Reduction of process scrap
14. Proper waste management
15. Efficient energy management
16. Profitable use of Human Resources

Of all the factors that influence the debt-equity mix or the capital structure choice, the most important factor is the nature of the company's business. Choosing an inappropriate capital structure for the type of business that the company is in is a recipe for disaster. Companies that embark on this path will soon experience financial distress or difficulty meeting their financial obligations. Due to the tax benefit that debt confers, short-sighted companies go on a borrowing binge. Soon the debt level becomes very large and unsustainable. A sudden slowdown of the economy or a downturn in the business, puts a debt-heavy company in a very precarious position. Debt servicing becomes very challenging. If this problem gets exacerbated, the company may be forced to file for bankruptcy. Corporate America is replete with examples of companies that were forced out of business due to excessive debt financing. Choosing a capital structure that is compatible with the nature of the industry and a cautious approach to debt financing would be prudent.

Corporate risk can be partitioned into business risk and financial risk. A company with high fixed operating costs has a high business risk. Besides, this would make the company's operating income highly sensitive to fluctuations in sales. This risk is measured by the Degree of Operating Leverage (DOL). If a firm has a high DOL, even a slight drop in sales will significantly reduce its operating income. Given this fact, if this firm borrows money, it would add financial risk to the business risk inherent in that business. This strategy would make the overall risk level unsustainable. Therefore, it is critically important for companies to choose a capital structure compatible with the type of company's business. While the proper capital structure can enhance shareholder value, the wrong one can destroy value.

An aggressive cost-reduction program is vital for growth. Cost reduction is not an ad hoc exercise. It is a participative program involving all employees. This program's success depends on the ability to identify cost-improvement areas and monitor them effectively for successful results. The objective of the program is to provide:

1. A systematic way to submit, analyze, evaluate, and implement proposals for cutting costs
2. Stimulate creative thinking in all areas of responsibility
3. Develop a more efficient and more economical operation
4. Measure participation and performance against division-wide plans for cost reduction

Training programs in the importance of finance, interpretation of figures, and the impact of their decisions, performance, and activities on the organizations' financial results are essential from a value creation perspective.

The cost reduction initiatives are the responsibility of every person in the organization. It is not a task to be relegated to a few individuals. There must be a companywide commitment and resolve to these initiatives successful. These initiatives should not be mere tokenism designed to impress the stock market. Cost consciousness must permeate all levels of the organization and must be woven into the operating plans. It must be a core part of the corporate credo. All employees must be sensitized to the importance of cost reduction measures. If the employees are convinced that these initiatives will ultimately benefit them personally, they will extend their wholehearted support. Therefore, making the employees aware of how these initiatives will benefit is a key task of management. Once the mindset of the employees in this regard is changed, implementation of these measures will become easier. In this context, it is important to note that the more the participants, the greater the flow of ideas, cost savings, and sense of achievement when the target is reached. This concept is a simple one. But to derive success, immense faith in it and attitudinal change is necessary. Dedication, determination, perseverance, and the ability to accept and work with others will undoubtedly lead to success. Once the cost improvement effort is channeled into formal activity, it can substantially reduce operating costs continuously and thereby enhance firm value. This program's success will depend the commitment of all the employees and the willingness of the management to invest resources in areas such as training programs to make this laudable growth, a reality.

We are living today in a world that is rapidly changing. Technology is changing, competition is becoming sharper, consumers have become discerning, and customer demands have become more exacting. However, many industrial establishments are engaged in mass production methods, large-scale mechanization, and large-scale investments. Therefore, it is a challenging task to ensure a reasonable rate of return on investments. Under these circumstances, the organization must be efficient, nimble, and agile to maintain its economic viability and ensure continued employment for its employees. It must also try to foresee the changes that are likely to happen in the marketplace in the near future and put in place a plan to respond to those changes.

Despite the large-scale devastation and destruction caused by World War II, Japan, Korea, and China have emerged as world leaders in many industries, such as automobiles, electronics, fiber optics, and heavy engineering, to name a few. Their focus has been on two issues: competitive performance and profitable use of human and other resources. Therefore, companies across industries must immediately focus on these aspects to improve their survival and growth margin.

Nowadays, companies in many parts of the world are carrying out a considerable amount of value engineering exercises to cut production costs and make their products more competitive, not just in the domestic market but also in the global markets. Furthermore, this goal must be pursued despite extreme scarcity and constraints concerning materials, power supply, and technology that may persist in many emerging countries. The increased cost of materials, energy, labor, and environmental controls significantly impact operations. Companies may face a limitation in obtaining a price increase from their customers for cost escalations. It will be a matter of concern if there is a substantial decline in the past few years' profitability. In this context, waste management has tremendous relevance in improving margins for survival and growth. Generally, the most significant saving in any operation is achieved by avoiding wasteful habits and practices. As customers continuously demand more products, more waste will likely be generated. Waste management, therefore, will have to be given the highest priority by the management. Savings obtained from avoiding waste or recycling, or using waste often induce better profitability than more sales. Anything that can be done to reduce operational costs by lowering non-productive expenditures such as waste of resources, waste disposal, salvage, and rectification work will improve margins appreciably. Therefore, organizations must look at waste reduction, resource recovery, and alternate uses for waste materials for money savings. In many emerging countries such as India, governmental restrictions on waste, discharges, and emissions, from entering water bodies and the atmosphere are increasing. Due to this reason, proper waste management has become a strategic imperative that has implications for value creation.

With the dumping areas for waste diminishing in many emerging countries due to land scarcity and transport costs increasing, reclamation and recycling waste must be considered a priority. However, excess waste often is generated from inadequate in-plant housekeeping procedures and operational slackness or deviations from laid down controls and practices in the business and manufacturing operations.

Building better awareness among the company's supervisors and operating personnel is needed to reduce material waste in all operations. Therefore, this should be a part of the routine training efforts. Most cost-reduction programs deal with equipment, workforce utilization, and process capacity utilization. However, waste reduction, recovery, and alternate use are rarely considered. Many innovative techniques have to be employed to prevent waste and discover constructive uses for the waste. Waste reduction should be continuously emphasized in the process and day-to-day operations. Companies will have to plan and budget for waste management as they do for capital expenditure for production equipment. For any program on waste management to be successful, it needs all its employees' wholehearted cooperation and dedication. In his context, the proper utilization of human resources is essential. Bringing about a change and approach to waste management and quality enhancement among middle-level managers is challenging but necessary. A change in the mindset of executives is required in this regard. The ultimate benefit of an effective waste management program is enhanced value creation. Therefore, the time, effort, and resources invested into these initiatives is worth it.

Internal Audit

In emerging markets, such as India, investments of large magnitude have been made in the last few decades to achieve rapid strides of industrialization. Only when such assets are employed efficiently, can they result in the country's economic prosperity. Hard work, purposeful planning, and faithful implementation are necessary for economic prosperity. In this task, every enterprise in the country should produce goods and services at economical costs. Therefore, scarce resources must be used effectively, especially in the current economic, hypercompetitive, and ever-changing global business environment. Every industrial unit has to work efficiently to achieve this objective. Therefore, in this endeavor, development of goals, plans, policies, systems, and procedures, and efficient management of industrial and business operations, is essential. Hence, a nimble, agile, and functional organizational structure that is compatible with the industry in which the company operates, should be designed and implemented.

Internal controls should be established for the successful accomplishment of the results. Elements of internal control are organization, system and procedures, policies, implementation, accounting and other records, performance standards, and reports. The internal control pattern will vary depending on the operations' size, personnel competency, organization structure, and control cost. For improving organizational efficiency, senior management looks upon the internal auditor for their assessment and evaluation of the effectiveness of the controls and their recommendations for guiding and directing the organization's destiny.

Statutory audits focus primarily on the external expression of an opinion on the true fairness of financial statements, which powerfully influence investment markets, governmental action, and management decisions. In comparison, an internal audit is an independent appraisal function established within an organization to examine and evaluate its activities as a service to the organization to improve efficiency, as well as compliance of legal procedures and risk management. In its narrow sense, such an audit is carried out by specialist staff. It concerns itself mainly with checking accounting transactions to quickly locate legal compliance and irregularities, discovering frauds and embezzlements, and property encroachment. In a broader sense, however, the internal audit's objective should be to assist the CEO and senior managers in an organization with analysis, appraisals, information, and recommendations concerning the activities reviewed for improving results. Internal audit should focus on (a) compliance with all statutory laws and procedures, (b) examination of the mechanisms which are used to control the operations and achieve objectives, (c) appraisal and evaluation of the adequacy and effectiveness of the control mechanism, and (d) report of the findings and constructive recommendations. It is the internal auditor's significant contribution that will enable the top management to control the future progress of the business better. The importance of internal audits is growing day by day. The scope for internal audits in any organization is extensive. Internal audits now encompass operational areas of a business. These areas include manufacturing operations, technology gaps, quality control, adequacy of systems and procedures in production, quality, and plant maintenance. Internal audit studies would improve operational effectiveness in diverse areas such as financial management, digitization, detection of cybercrimes, personnel administration, marketing operations, legal compliance, and the possibility of embezzlement and fraud. Significant decisions on large-scale investments are taken based on certain assumptions. One or more premises in the project may not materialize and expose it to severe risks. Project implementation calls for a high degree of coordination to integrate civil works activities, machinery procurement, raising financial resources, obtaining government approvals and clearances, erections, installation, and commissioning. Periodic internal audit studies will considerably help monitor the project effectively without time or cost overruns.

Persons actively engaged in the day-to-day humdrum of industrial activity may not devote enough time to examining whether the resources under their control are being economically and efficiently utilized. Internal audit activity can be directed to studies such as review of operating standards, utilization of facilities, manning strength, rework expenses, rejects and disposal thereof, material utilization, unnecessary and unproductive work, and pollution control.

The complexity in organizations has led to the development of a systems approach for organizational and operational efficiency. This strategy helps improve the understanding of the importance of the various activities, objectives, duties, and responsibilities of individuals and helps maintain consistency in approach, and assists in reviewing the action taken, resulting in the success or failure of any particular task. A system can only be successful if it is faithfully adhered to by the persons operating it. Periodic audits of such systems will ensure that the systems are meticulously followed and adequately implemented. It will also help ascertain and redesign such systems' adequacy to suit the changing needs.

In an industry engaged in the mass production of goods of varying variety, grades, and specifications, it can be challenging to ensure output quality. The company's image and credibility will depend on the standards of quality the company is consistently able to maintain. Detailed processes and quality control systems and procedures are laid down for the purpose. Regular audit reviews will ensure such procedures are followed properly, highlight deviations from prescribed norms or standards, and update them where necessary.

We are living in a world of rapid and tremendous technological changes. Technological obsolescence is one of the biggest threats facing businesses today. Plant and equipment installed a few years ago may not produce goods to suit the customers' changing demands. The knowledge and skills of people working in an establishment may also not be relevant to the changing needs. It is necessary, therefore, to have an audit to determine if there is any obsolescence in technology, facilities, and the workforce. Such audits will help management take suitable action to update technology or modernize facilities or designs, and conduct intensive training and development programs.

Apart from the routine functions of verification of the existence of assets, an internal audit program should cover a review of the systems and procedures and precautions taken to safeguard the assets from various types of losses due to theft, fire, storage, natural deterioration, illegal occupation or encroachment, safety and protection of vital records, deeds, and documents. With digitization, the security of designs and drawings, critical and sensitive information, is essential and challenging.

Accumulating raw material inventory, components, work-in-progress and finished stocks, represents funds lying dormant, resulting in financial losses. It results in a loss of interest and in cash being locked up, which otherwise would have been available for better utilization. This area affords tremendous scope for the internal auditor to improve efficiency. Studies on using materials, purchase procedures, inventory levels, and slow-moving and non-moving items will help reduce and control inventories. Similarly, the accumulation of work-in-progress and finished stocks on the shop floor merits the internal auditor's special attention. Studies may reveal imbalances in facilities, incorrect scheduling of jobs, imbalances in the output of a few items leading to incomplete sets for production, and lack of inter-departmental coordination.

To be effective, internal auditors must have good business experience, job knowledge, tact, pleasant manners, analytical ability, innovative approach, and written and oral communication skills to put across their views convincingly. An essential factor that should be considered in internal audits is the constructive approach to improve organizational efficiency. On no account should an internal audit be used to settle personal rivalries in an organization. The audit team should comprise multidisciplinary experts with good common sense, knowledge, tact, and communication skills.

Coping With a Recession

The word "recession" is a dreaded word for most CEOs. However, a company can cope with a recession through innovative strategies and subsequently thrive.

A recession is defined as three consecutive quarters of negative GDP growth (Gross Domestic Product). Economic shocks, financial panic, or medical pandemics can trigger it. Economic activity contracts during a recession. Recession causes a fall in demand and, thereby, revenue. Companies downsize their operations. Consequently, unemployment increases, and the government's welfare spending goes up.

Recession makes the future outlook uncertain and makes companies put off capital investments and product innovations as the focus is on survival. Recessions do damage companies. However, the decline of a company is not inevitable during a recession. There are ways by which companies can fight the specter of recession and emerge successful.

If the management foresees the onset of a recession, they should first examine whether they are overleveraged. If the answer to this critical question is yes, steps should be taken immediately to deleverage the company. A recession is likely to affect all companies. However, companies most hurt during a downturn are the ones that have high debt levels. When revenue shrinks during a recession, a company with a high debt level will find that the interest burden will become a more significant proportion of the reduced revenue level. Servicing the mandatory interest payment obligation will become challenging. The company will struggle to make those payments. Then it will start experiencing a state called "financial distress." If financial distress worsens, it could lead to bankruptcy and liquidation. Companies in financial distress are forced to cut costs very aggressively, usually through massive layoffs that can deleteriously affect employee morale and productivity. Besides, massive layoffs could affect the company's DNA and cause lasting damage from which the company may never recover.

Therefore, deleveraging a company before the onset of a recession is critically essential. Before deciding to deleverage, the management should examine the company's existing debt level and determine whether it is appropriate, given the nature of the company's business. The management should also benchmark the company's debt level with the industry average to determine whether it is in line or out of line with its peers in the industry.

One way of deleveraging the company is to issue common stock and use the proceeds to buy back debt. This strategy will bring about a rapid change in the capital structure. Another alternative is to use corporate cash (if available) to pay down debt to the extent possible. In addition, selling assets that are unutilized or underutilized and using the proceeds to pay down the debt would be a prudent strategy. In this regard, the bottom line is that starting sooner than later concerning deleveraging, is better. This approach means that companies should reduce their debt level before it becomes apparent that the economy is in recession.

The organizational structure also has an impact on the ability of a company to navigate during a recession. A centralized organizational structure is appropriate because it provides a macro view of the organization and helps them make tough decisions quickly. However, a decentralized organizational structure helps a firm better cope with a recession because of local information access, enabling companies to adapt to changing conditions much faster. In addition, critical operational and product-portfolio decisions can be quickly made in a decentralized organization. An organization with a rigid, hierarchical structure may be sclerotic concerning decision-making in a rapidly changing business environment. The bottom line is that the organizational structure chosen by a company should be compatible with the nature of the industry that the company is in and its value-creating objectives.

Layoffs cannot usually be avoided in a recession. However, companies should rely more on operational efficiency improvements than layoffs to emerge from a downturn successfully. Some CEOs subscribe to the "slash and burn school of management" and view layoffs as a panacea for corporate ills. However, this provides only a short-term boost. Ultimately, massive layoffs are demoralizing for employees and affect their productivity. It is costly because when the company decides to hire again, it has to invest many inexpensive hiring and training resources.

However, layoffs are not the only option for reducing labor costs. Through innovative approaches, labor costs can be lowered without resorting to layoffs. The strategies include reduced work hours, furloughs, and performance-based pay. These strategies can help vulnerable companies retain more of their workforce during a recession and assist them in quickly ramping up the business after the recession. With furloughs and reduced work hours, companies can adopt a targeted approach to cost reduction instead of across-the-board layoffs, which can damage morale, lower productivity, and force talented employees to seek employment elsewhere.

Investing in new technology during a recession would be a wise strategy. The opportunity cost of investing in new technology in a recession is lower than during good times. Besides, technology can make a company more transparent, flexible, agile, and efficient.

Technology will cost less during a recession than during a boom time. Companies should also invest in data analytics during a downturn. Enhanced analytics can help management better understand the business and the emerging trends, how the recession impacts the business, and the areas where there is scope for operational improvements. Investments in information technology can help companies become more agile and better enable them to handle the uncertainty and vicissitudes caused by a recession.

In summary, a well-thought-out strategy before the onset of a recession will enable a company to emerge much more robust than its peers from a business downtown.

Downsizing

Cost-cutting, through downsizing, has been viewed as a panacea during tough times, especially during a recession. For example, during the global financial crisis of 2008/2009, thousands of companies resorted to downsizing as a desperate measure to survive. Many of these companies did not survive despite laying off thousands of workers.

Companies downsize during tough times and sometimes when they are healthy too. The goal is to create a leaner, nimble, and agile organization that can quickly respond to changes in the business environment.

A debate has been raging for quite some time on whether downsizing is good for the company in the long run. There is a school of thought that downsizing may actually increase the probability of the company going bankrupt.

There are many adverse effects of downsizing. It has a highly negative impact on employee morale. The stress caused to the remaining employees due to downsizing will likely adversely impact their productivity. It may also negatively impinge customer satisfaction.

We live today in a knowledge-based world. Knowledge is a critical asset. Employees who are laid off due to downsizing carry their knowledge with them. Finding new persons with the same knowledge as the ones who departed is challenging. In other words, downsizing leads to knowledge depletion. Also, the workload for the remaining employees in a downsized organization increases. This fact makes it very difficult for them to acquire new skills and competencies, which may be essential for the firm to remain competitive. In addition, downsizing negatively affects employees' trust in the top management and the company. This fact will, in turn, affect innovation and competitiveness and put the firm on the path to bankruptcy. While downsizing may provide some short-term cost-reduction benefits, its long-term effects may be disastrous. It is likely to lead to value destruction.

The downsizing decision, therefore, is a trade-off. The management must weigh the short-term cost savings with the deleterious long-term effects. One factor that may mitigate the harmful effects of downsizing is the presence of intangible resources. Effective deployment of existing intangible resources, such as the knowledge of the remaining employees is likely to help in this regard. The management must therefore resist the temptation to eliminate intangible resources.

In summary, downsizing is not a panacea for an organization's ailments. It must be resorted to only after careful thought and planning. Simultaneously, the firm's existing intangible resources must be preserved, enhanced, and carefully redeployed to protect the firm from the negative consequences of downsizing.

The Covid Pandemic
and Its Aftermath

The COVID pandemic had a profound effect on business and changed life as we know it. Therefore, companies have been forced to re-evaluate their growth opportunities, modify their business model, and redeploy their capital astutely.

The pandemic caused a change in customers' habits. Identifying and evaluating the shifts in habits before the competitors realize them has become a strategic imperative.

Therefore, in the post-COVID world, companies need to assess the possible ramifications of emerging trends and identify the business opportunities that are likely to emanate. The key is for companies to identify and understand emerging habits and pivot quickly to leverage the trends.

For example, brick-and-mortar retailers were walloped by the pandemic. This fact has accelerated the trend toward online shopping. Consumers did not need to shop at a physical store during a pandemic when they could shop from the safety of their homes. This trend has become the new normal, and retailers must adapt quickly. Otherwise, their survival will be at stake.

Then, companies need to determine whether the trends are likely to be short-term or long-term, whether they already existed or have arisen since the inception of the pandemic. This strategy requires a careful examination and analysis of relevant data from a multitude of sources.

Once a company has identified its future growth opportunities, it must modify its business model to capitalize on them. In addition, it must keep track of the shifts in demand and supply in its industry. For example, the relationship between the United States (under the Trump administration) and China reached its nadir. This development created challenges for many U.S. firms concerning their supply chain as they depended on the supply of critical components from China. The tensions with China have continued under the present Biden administration.

The COVID pandemic profoundly affected the supply chain of many U.S. manufacturing companies. Companies are still struggling to cope with the new normal brought about by the pandemic. Modifying the business to this new normal would require companies to be clear about how they create and provide value, whom they should partner with, and who the target consumers are. Companies that aspire to become a market leader must clearly define how they wish to compete. They must decide whether to focus on product innovation, superior customer service, excellent product quality, or expanding market share. It would benefit a company to identify its core competence in this regard.

Once a company defines its market clearly, it can effectively focus on its target customer. Determining the market requires a dispassionate assessment of the capabilities as well as the core competence of the company. There must also be a thorough needs assessment of the target customer. The company must also be clear about what it will not do.

In addition, despite the financial challenges caused by the pandemic which are still continuing, companies should be willing to increase their investment in technology. These investments should be targeted at new growth opportunities to optimize the benefit from these investments. Companies should also deploy their capital to those business segments with higher growth and return opportunities. This strategy would be prudent, given the fact that the pandemic has forced companies to operate in a resource-constrained environment.

There is a tendency to hoard cash during an economic downturn. However, the crisis can be turned into an opportunity to reinvent the business model. This strategy may require aggressive capital investment. Of course, this strategy will be fraught with risk. But it is worth taking this risk. The capital allocation decision should be dynamic. After due diligence, capital should be quickly deployed into promising projects.

There has been a paradigm shift in the nature of work due to the COVID pandemic. The old ways of doing business are not relevant anymore. Companies must adjust to this new normal. In the post-pandemic world, a significant majority of companies will be combining remote and onsite working. Productivity has increased during the pandemic. The sustainability of the productivity gains will depend on the steps' companies take to alleviate employees' anxiety regarding the remote and onsite work that the management decides on. Enhancing and sustaining productivity increases will be possible only if companies provide their employees with a nurturing work environment where coaching, mentoring, idea sharing, and coworking occur. Keeping the employees connected, even if they are operating from different remote locations, is a crucial element that will determine the success of the hybrid work model in the post-pandemic world.

The pandemic has accelerated the pace of digital transformation in many industries. Enhancing customer experience has become even more critical in this new digital world. Consumers have a multitude of choices today. Given this fact, they will do business with companies that provide them with a convenient, seamless, and enhanced customer experience.

The pandemic has forced companies to adopt new ways of working. Companies have been forced to disband silos and erase boundaries in the organization. Technology has also been adopted at a much faster rate than before. The shift toward digital products and services has accelerated. Decision-making has become much more decentralized. This development has spawned a new generation of potential leaders. Cross-functional empowered teams have become the norm, not an exception. Customer experience enhancement has become of paramount importance and a strategic imperative. It has also become the vital key to value creation.

The COVID pandemic has forced companies to become more agile and nimble. There is now grudging acceptance that only such organizations can survive the onslaught of competition in an increasingly complex global business environment.

Initially, when the pandemic hit, companies simultaneously faced many challenges, such as reduced demand, office closures due to lockdowns, disruptions in the supply chain, and resource constraints. Companies were forced to operate with less of everything. Companies had to define the most critical objectives they hoped to accomplish clearly. Defining the corporate purpose became a strategic imperative. A well-defined corporate purpose enabled quick decision-making.

Companies that have adapted to the new normal in the post-pandemic period are likely to prosper while those that do not do so will fade away. Companies must learn to navigate a turbulent post-pandemic world that is fraught with uncertainty.

While defining a corporate purpose is a laudable objective, it is insufficient. Processes must be implemented to facilitate the attainment of the corporate purpose.

During the pandemic, visionary business leaders realized the importance of creating and deploying cross-functional teams to achieve specific outcomes. They also discovered that a traditional hierarchical organization can impede quick decision-making and that a flatter, decentralized organizational structure, with the management at the frontlines, will facilitate a rapid response to changes in the business environment. In addition, empowering teams at the front lines will help in the resolution of customer complaints in an expeditious manner. This strategy will also prevent minor problems from snowballing into major crises. Faster decision-making is possible only when frontline teams are empowered. Technology is a vital element in bringing about the success of this empowerment. Technology is being used for customer experience enhancement as this area is the key to success in a highly competitive global business environment.

Companies have learned many lessons from the pandemic. They were forced to change their operating model. Many of them are now looking to make these changes permanent. The experience gained during the pandemic gives companies the confidence to keep reinventing the business model and continue carrying out the transformations necessary to keep the organization agile, nimble, and capable of meeting the competition head-on. Therefore, companies will unlikely go back to the old ways of doing business.

As companies adapt to the new normal caused by the pandemic, they must cast away their traditional thinking, adopt a bold new approach, and seize opportunities as they emerge.

Leadership Challenges in the Post-Pandemic World

The COVID-19 pandemic has had a profound impact on various aspects of business. Business leaders have had to significantly increase the scope of their decision-making and learn how to operate in a resource-constrained environment. Companies that have successfully adapted to the vicissitudes of the post-pandemic world have thrived while their nimble and agile rivals have pushed aside those who could not do so. The leaders at these successful companies have expanded their skills to encompass a wide range of areas.

Business leaders who wish to succeed in this rapidly changing and complex global business environment need to take a step back from the mundane task of running the business and visualize how the business world will likely evolve in the near future and what role their company will play in this new world. They need to be strategic thinkers and visionaries with the foresight to anticipate changes before they happen. They need to make **value creation** the **central theme** of all activities and continually explore new ways of creating value. They also need to be excellent executors and not mere visionaries. They need to map out the specific operational steps to translate their vision into a reality. Given the dynamic changes in the marketplace, flawless execution has become a critical strategic imperative and sine qua non for value creation.

The post-pandemic business world requires leaders to have the courage to make bold decisions. It also requires humility and an inclusive style of leadership. It is also essential for leaders to have the ability to bring together people from diverse backgrounds. Since good ideas may emanate from anywhere in the organization, leaders should be willing to listen to employees who put forth ideas and also give credit where it is due.

Today, technology permeates virtually every aspect of business across industries. Therefore, the technological challenges faced by the company must be delegated to more than just the CIO or a person with a similar rank. Leaders have to keep abreast of the latest trends in technology and how they will likely impact their business. They also need to understand the impact of technology on people in general and employees and customers in particular. A humanistic approach to leadership will pay rich dividends.

Having clarity of purpose and establishing a corporate credo that captures the company's values will help the leaders steer the organization in the right direction and achieve the value creation objectives, regardless of the vicissitudes of the changes in the business environment. Leaders also need to create a conducive environment in the organization to foster innovation.

Given the uncertainties of the post-pandemic business world, leaders must be able to "build bridges" and bring various stakeholders together to achieve predetermined value-creation objectives. This strategy is possible only when leaders establish trust and integrity and use these as beacons to guide their actions and interactions with others.

Leaders also need to have a global mindset and source talent from whichever part of the world it is available. At the same time, leaders need to address the needs of the local communities. Enhanced customer service is essential to attract and retain customers.

In summary, navigating the turbulent post-pandemic business environment will require great skill and dexterity. Leaders who aspire to succeed in this new world must equip themselves with the necessary skills and develop a growth mindset grounded on the bedrock of humility, integrity, trust, and commitment.

Joint Ventures and Partnerships

Although the COVID pandemic has largely abated in most countries, it is still prevalent in some countries such as China which is struggling to cope with a massive new wave of COVID infections. This pandemic caused a severe strain on the financial health of companies around the world. There is hope on the horizon. However, to take advantage of the economic upswing that is likely to happen soon, companies must restructure operations, redeploy resources, and re-evaluate business models. Joint ventures and partnerships may help companies rebound from the after-effects of a recession much faster. Numerous joint ventures and partnerships exist in industries such as oil and gas, automotive, and pharmaceuticals. Pfizer and BioNTech established an alliance in March 2020 to develop a COVID-19 vaccine jointly. In December 2020, their vaccine received EUA (emergency use authorization) from the U.S. Food and Drug Administration (FDA) and has been administered to millions worldwide. Therefore, if properly structured and administered, a joint venture can result in a mutually beneficial relationship. Companies are usually forced to operate in a resource-constrained environment during an economic downturn. A joint venture or partnership can alleviate the problem of paucity of resources. Sharing of resources can foster innovation and help strengthen both companies.

Existing joint ventures will face many challenges when there is an economic downturn. These include a revenue drop, supply chain disruption, market reduction decline, and difficulty accessing credit. Therefore, the joint ventures may need to be restructured. There must be a serious effort to cut costs judiciously, decrease working capital requirements, explore new financing options, and fully leverage government relief programs and subsidies. This strategy will require a proactive approach from the board. Ultimately, the success of a joint venture depends on the involvement and acumen of board directors.

Joint ventures must identify opportunities to secure funds from various sources, including state-owned companies, private equity (PE), and sovereign-wealth funds. They can use these funds to strengthen their operations and seek new business opportunities. Furthermore, some investors, like PE firms, can bring skills and competencies that will prove invaluable to the joint venture, such as expertise in cost reduction and experience in M&A.

A joint venture operates within an ecosystem of suppliers, lenders, and customers. An economic downturn is an excellent time for a joint venture to think "out of the box" and structure creative commercial arrangements with these stakeholders.

A joint venture should also consider insourcing some functions currently provided by an owner company. This approach may be more cost-effective for the joint venture.

Right-sizing a company through judicious cost-cutting is critical during a business downturn. However, massive, mindless, and myopic cost-cutting and layoffs can be detrimental to the organization and ultimately result in value destruction. Establishing a joint venture with a company that has expertise in cost reduction could result in cost synergies that would be very helpful.

In summary, companies must seek new, innovative ways to survive and prosper even when there is an economic downturn.

Future Trends

The COVID pandemic and its aftermath has changed the lives of people around the world. Many people have been subjected to tremendous personal and professional struggles since 2020. The pandemic has also caused a paradigm shift in how employers support employees. Employees have belatedly realized that getting more involved in the personal lives of their employees and helping them cope with their challenges builds trust and loyalty and allows employees to perform at a higher level. Therefore, in the years to come, we can expect employees to invest more resources in supporting the physical, mental, and financial health of their employees.

Traditionally, companies have shied away from taking positions on societal and political issues. This approach is likely to change in the future. Employees like to work for organizations whose values align with their own. There is an expectation among employees that they would like their employers to get more involved in social issues.

The trend toward working from home will continue to gather pace in the near future. Many leading companies like Apple and Google have already allowed some employees to work from home permanently. The need for lavish and expensive offices has become a moot point. Allowing employees to work from home is seen as a cost-reduction measure and a way to retain talent. Women tend to shoulder a disproportionate share of family responsibilities. Therefore, it is likely that more women would prefer to work from home than men. However, because of the misplaced perception that office workers are more productive than their counterparts who work from a remote location, companies may likely give in-office workers a higher raise than remotely located workers. Since more men than women prefer to be in-house workers, they are more likely to receive higher raises than women. Therefore, wage inequity may rise in the years to come.

Companies have been using various tools to monitor employees who work from home. Since this is intrusive and could infringe on privacy, new regulations could likely be put in place in the near future to restrict the monitoring of employees.

Companies have realized that internal talent is their greatest resource and that they should use this talent most efficiently. Therefore, it is likely that companies will actively encourage and facilitate internal mobility so that employees can be deployed to the areas where the organizational needs are the greatest. The compensation offered to the employees for this internal redeployment will likely be multi-faceted to retain employees with critically important skills. Opportunities will also be provided to employees who wish to upgrade their skills.

Historically, companies have followed the traditional paths of sourcing talent. Companies now need to diversify their talent pipelines to help meet their talent requirements. Therefore. in the future, companies will likely rely less on formal academic credentials and more on skills that a potential employee has. Companies will evaluate whether candidates have the skills to perform a particular role. The hiring of people with nontraditional backgrounds will increase in the future.

Managers are considered to be the critical liaison between the employees and the top leadership of a company. They are likely to face increasing pressure in the near future to satisfy the demands of the different stakeholders. Balancing competing expectations from the management and the employees will be challenging. Leading companies will likely provide support and training to help managers cope with these challenges.

The COVID pandemic brought about a paradigm shift in how people work. The focus has now shifted from time to output. Employees are measured by their production, not by time spent on the job. This fact requires employers to offer their employees more flexibility regarding working hours. This policy has become a strategic necessity.

Since vaccination dramatically reduces the chances of contracting COVID and other similar diseases, employers have been investing resources into providing the vaccines to their employees and encouraging them to get vaccinated. This trend is likely to continue since companies have realized the need to adopt a proactive approach to coping with potential health emergencies. The adage "a healthy workforce is a productive workforce" is very true.

The COVID pandemic had a deleterious effect on many employees' mental and physical health. This fact is negatively impinging on their productivity. Employees have to contend with the emotional and physical impacts of the pandemic. Therefore, we expect companies to spend more on health services in general and mental health services in the years to come.

Employers are likely to source talent from outside temporarily as the required skill set may not be available internally. So, we expect the number of gig or part-time workers to increase in the near future. Talent can be sourced from remote locations globally. As these workers are not full-time employees, they usually do not have to be paid the regular benefits. So sourcing talent from outside the organization on an "as needed" basis makes financial sense too.

Historically, states have provided tax incentives to companies to relocate. What is likely to happen now is that states may offer tax incentives for individuals to relocate to their jurisdiction. Given the trend toward working from home, what has now become very important is not only where companies are located but also where skilled individuals are located.

During the past few years, nimble and agile new entrants like Uber have disrupted many traditional industries. This trend will accelerate soon, transforming many industries and creating new ones.

The COVID pandemic profoundly affected business and has changed life as we knew it. Therefore, companies must re-evaluate their growth opportunities, modify their business model, and redeploy their capital astutely.

The pandemic has also caused a change in consumer habits. Identifying and evaluating these shifts in habits before the competition realizes them has become a strategic imperative.

The COVID pandemic had a significant impact on labor markets globally during 2020. Millions of people were laid off while others had to quickly adapt to working from home. Workers deemed essential to work onsite had to adjust to the new safety protocols to reduce the coronavirus transmission. In the post-pandemic world, jobs involving high levels of physical proximity will likely see more significant transformation. These areas include healthcare, personal care, hospitality, onsite customer service, and travel.

Onsite customer service includes workers interacting with customers in banks, post offices, and retail stores. Due to the need to maintain social distancing to avoid the spread of the highly contagious coronavirus and its emerging variants as well as other communicable diseases, some work in this area has migrated to digital platforms. It will likely remain so for the foreseeable future.

The pandemic severely impacted the hospitality and travel industry. Many leisure venues closed down in 2020. Airline schedules were also severely curtailed as countries imposed strict entry restrictions to prevent the spread of the virus. Business travel also fell sharply as companies opted for virtual meetings instead of face-to-face interactions. There has been a rebound in the hospitality and travel sectors, especially since 2022. This fact is evidenced by the significant increase in the passenger load factor in many airlines operating long-haul routes. Hotel occupancy rates, especially branded hotels, have risen sharply. This fact is a welcome trend for hotels and airlines, which had been hit very severely after the onset of the COVID pandemic.

The computer-based office work area requires only a limited amount of human interactions and has seen the most significant transition to remote working.

The pandemic has had minimal impact on the outdoor production and maintenance areas as these jobs have low proximity and interactions with others and take place outdoors.

The pandemic has accelerated the shift to flexible workspaces. This trend will reduce the demand for office space. This fact will negatively impact the commercial real estate sector. It will also result in declining restaurants and public transportation demand in downtown areas.

With the sharp increase in remote work, the demand for business travel will likely reduce. There is now increased acceptance of virtual meetings. Such meetings have now become the norm, not an exception. The decline in business travel is likely to affect airlines adversely. The impact on airlines is expected to have a ripple effect and impinge on other related sectors such as airports, hospitality, and food service.

The pandemic resulted in a significant spike in e-commerce transactions and other online activities. This trend is likely to continue for the foreseeable future. This trend has also resulted in substantial growth in delivery, transportation, and warehouse jobs.

During the pandemic, virtual transactions such as telemedicine, online banking, and video streaming took off significantly. The current post-pandemic period is likely to dip in these transactions, but they will remain well above pre-pandemic levels.

In the post-pandemic period, companies are likely to step up their investment in automation and AI. But there is growing concern that emerging technologies such as AI may be used to violate employees' privacy and surreptitiously gather personal and private information. This trend portends a looming privacy crisis. HR managers must prioritize transparency regarding how the company collects, uses, and stores employee information and allow employees to opt out of the data-gathering process if they find it too intrusive and objectionable.

There is a growing trend to use AI in the hiring and promotion processes. To avoid employee backlash, HR managers need to be more transparent about using AI and disseminating audit data, and allowing employees to opt out of the AI-led processes.

A significant negative impact of the pandemic is likely to fall on workers engaged in sectors such as food service and customer sales. Therefore, a steep drop in food service and customer service jobs is expected in the near future.

Jobs in the healthcare sector are likely to increase. This trend will be fueled by aging populations in the Western World, China, and Japan and the increased focus on health due to the pandemic. Maintaining a healthy workforce has become a strategic imperative. There is also now a widespread acceptance of the fact that good health is a crucial determinant of productivity.

Therefore, companies need to assess the possible ramifications of emerging trends and identify the business opportunities likely to emanate from those trends. The key is for companies to identify and understand the emerging habits of consumers and pivot quickly to leverage the habits.

Companies that spot emerging trends early and capitalize on them will thrive. Those that don't will wither and die. Companies will be faced with two stark choices: **Adapt or die.**

In a competitive labor market, employers must distinguish themselves from their competitors and project themselves as preferred organizations that provide a conducive and harmonious work environment that offers opportunities for personal growth and professional development. This strategy is the key to attracting and retaining talent.

Conclusion

In the various sections of this handbook, we have touched upon multiple management aspects that must be treated simultaneously for organizations' stability and growth. For an organization to "dare to be different," innovation, new technology, continuous training, enhancing customer experience, systems and procedures, fair and consistent human relations policies, and ethical business practices are essential. In compliance with a country's laid-down laws, research in every activity area, including digitization, and leadership with a healthy attitude, is necessary. We are sure these guidelines would enable employees in any organization to navigate skillfully and lead their companies to growth, progress, and success even in turbulent times. In addition, we believe that even companies in the developing world, can "dare to be different" and become truly world class firms who can effectively compete against their global peers.

Index

A

achievable targets, setting, 195
acquisitions, iii, 7, 46, 110–11, 113, 115–17, 119, 155
activities, corporate restructuring, 119
adaptability, iv, 134–37
agile organizations, iv, 4, 10, 139, 142–44, 262
algorithms, 59–60, 63, 68, 70, 185–86, 189–93
Alibaba, 140
Amazon, 66, 81, 83, 90, 102–3, 105
analysis, 96
 sentiment, 181, 186–87
analytics, 69
Anderson, Chris, 92
Applicant Tracking System (ATS), 192
applications, incorrect, 70
audit, organizational resilience, 43

B

bandwidth constraints, 62
bargaining value, 112
big data, 11, 66, 82, 93–94, 162, 181–83, 188–89, 192
blended approach, 18
Boring Company, 5
brand building, 84–85
brand loyalty, 57, 74, 170, 172, 274

Brazil, Russia, India, and China (BRIC), 2
Brexit process, 2
British Energy Group, 116
business environment, 18, 23, 43, 58, 110, 134–36, 141, 146, 148, 172, 222, 245, 262, 268, 270
 global, 2, 5, 18, 35, 140, 174
businesses, 1, 8–11, 161, 198, 228, 245, 254, 256, 260–61, 264–69, 277–78
business ethics, 132
business goals, 67, 69
business model resilience, 43
business objectives, 95
business transformation, 90–93, 98, 101

C

capital, 50, 52–54, 104, 120, 152, 220, 232, 247, 264, 266, 277
carbon footprint, 64, 87
cause-focused purpose, 27
Centers of Excellence (COE), 162
change management, iv, 146–48
chatbots, 188, 191–92
Chick-fil-A, 140
chief executive officer (CEO), 5–6, 8, 10, 42, 58, 75, 77–78, 87–89, 125–28, 142, 144–47, 149–50, 152–53, 155–56,

management, human resource, 199–200

management committees, iv, 127

management complexity, 107

managerial efficiency, v, 229

managers, 12, 31–32, 47, 96, 117, 127–28, 135, 143, 160–63, 167, 174–75, 194–99, 204–5, 210, 212, 217–18, 228, 234, 243, 275–76

manufacturing, 221

margins, 52, 55, 85, 229, 237, 244, 246, 251

Mars Mission, 6, 30

M&A strategy, 117

McNamara, Robert, 199

medical devices, 62–64

mergers, 110, 113, 117, 119, 155

metrics, 94–95, 128, 162

Microsoft Azure, 105

middle-level managers, 47, 161, 252

mission statement, 125

Mittal Steel-Arcelor deal, 116

Morita, Akio, 6

motivation, iv, 26, 35, 130, 194, 210, 217

Musk, Elon, 5

N

National Institutes of Health (NIH), 65

Netflix, 5, 185

network, extremely high, scalable, 62

Neuralink, 5

neural networks, 184, 191–92

Nirma, 21

Nokia, 115

North American Free Trade Agreement (NAFTA), 2

Norvig, Peter, 188

O

open business transformation, 92

operational resilience, 42

organic growth, 7, 10, 110

organization, 7

organizational agility, iv, 139, 144, 146

organizational capabilities, iii, 34, 36–37

organizational culture, iv, 76, 154–55, 180

organizational effectiveness, 32, 152, 160, 194, 199–200, 205, 208, 210–11, 233

organizational efficiency, 161, 163, 253, 257

organizational health, iv, 149–52

organizational resilience, 43

organizational structure, 25, 79, 130, 143–44, 225, 259–60

outcomes, 96

overleveraged firm, 119

over-the-counter drugs, 98–99

P

pain points, 96

paradigm shift, 25, 100, 134, 146, 172, 174, 179, 266, 274, 276

partnerships, v, 29, 35, 272

PayPal, 5

perception management, iii, 84–85

performance improvement, 128–29, 149

performers, 10, 35

personal goals, encouraging, 196

Philippines, 179

planning, 228
  succession, iv, 206

potential leaders, 162, 166–67, 267

Precision Medicine Initiative (PMI), 65

privacy, 43, 62, 83, 104, 106, 108, 275, 279

private equity (PE), 273

product development, v, 131, 194, 211, 221, 227–28

productivity, 231–32, 235, 241

purposeful leadership, 172–73

purpose statement, 26, 27, 79

Q

quality, 234, 236, 238–39

quality control, 131, 205, 236, 240

R

radio-frequency identification (RFID), 63

Ranbaxy, 115

R&D, 17–18, 56, 100, 131, 225–27

realization value, 112–13

recession, 2, 49, 117, 258–62, 272

reinforcement learning, 185

remote monitoring, 72–73

reputational resilience, 43

resilience, 41–42, 44, 59, 144

resource consumption, 4

responsibility award, 213

restructuring strategies, 122

Return on Invested Capital (ROIC), 85

revenue, 4, 9, 42, 55–57, 75, 85, 153, 258, 272

rewards, 27, 31–32, 47, 49, 99, 139, 150–51, 167, 197, 212–13

risk-averse mentality, 53

Russell, Stuart, 188

Russia, 2

S

sagacious strategist, 30

Sarbanes Oxley Act (SOX), 45

scalability, 60, 70, 102, 104

seasonal sales, 121

security, 60, 62–63, 72–73, 102, 104, 108, 132, 160, 184, 256

segmentation strategy, 94

shareholder value, 43, 45, 116, 249

Shareholder Value Added (SVA), 47

Sher, Robert, 114

Skype Technologies, 115

sluggish sales, 120–21

smart cars, 72

smart thermostats, 71

Solar City, 5

Sony, 6

SpaceX, 5

speed, 182

sponsors, 67

stakeholders, 24, 26–28, 43, 76, 126, 138, 146, 172, 225, 273, 275 stock market, 27, 45, 49, 85–86, 99, 191

stock returns, 113

strategic imperative, iv, 174

strategy

  customer-experience-enhancing, 82–83

  purpose-driven, 24–28, 87–89

strategy execution, iii, 31, 33, 57

strategy formulation, successful, 29

streamlining, 140, 143

successful companies, 10, 24, 36–37, 55–56, 134–35, 139, 269

Sun Pharma, 115

sustainability, iii, 16, 41, 49, 51, 87–88, 100, 266

T

talents, hiring, iv, 179

Tata Steel, 115

team spirit, 127, 132, 197, 212, 217

teamwork, iv, 7, 202, 208–9, 222

technological advancements, 91. *See also* smart cars; smart thermostats

technological obsolescence, 132, 256

technological resilience, 42–43

technology, 4, 60, 219–20, 250

  digital, 1, 4, 11, 41

Tesla Motors, 5, 72

top-down approach, 167

top management, 18, 24, 29–30, 34, 36, 49, 57, 128, 134, 137, 146, 149–50, 154–56, 158–59, 167, 225–26, 236, 254, 263

training, 203–4, 249

training programs, specialized, 204–5

transformation, digital, 10, 62, 64, 266

Trans-Pacific Partnership (TPP), 2

trust, 37, 40, 48, 50–51, 76–77, 82–84, 91–92, 127, 130, 135, 147, 157, 160, 164, 168, 170, 172, 175, 212, 214, 263, 274

Twitter, 5

U

underleveraged firm, 120

United States, 2, 45, 63, 92, 265

V

valuations, 111–12

value, 112, 182

value destruction, 40, 98, 112–15, 117, 263, 273

value estimations, 112

variety, 182

vehicle identification numbers (VINs), 61

vendors, 61, 63, 77, 108

ventures, joint, 110, 272–73

veracity, 182

Verizon Wireless, 116

virtual communities, 91

visionary leaders, 40, 137–38, 154, 268

Vodafone, 116

volume, 182

www.ingramcontent.com/pod-product-compliance
Lightning Source LLC
LaVergne TN
LVHW041203050326
832903LV00020B/433